From BORDER CROSSINGS to CAMPAIGN TRAIL

Chronicle of a Latina in Politics

by Emma Sepúlveda

Azul Editions
MCMXCVIII

The poems that appear in this book were first published in
Spain by Torremozas in *Tiempo cómplice del tiempo*, 1989.
They also appeared in my book *Death to Silence/Muerte al
silencio* published by Arte Público, 1997.

Published by
Azul Editions
7804 Sycamore Drive
Falls Church, VA 22042
USA
email: azulpress@aol.com

ISBN 1-885214-12-X

Library of Congress Catalog Number: 98-72737

Printed in the United States of America

First Edition
10 9 8 7 6 5 4 3 2 1

from BORDER CROSSINGS

to CAMPAIGN TRAIL

Chronicle of a Latina in Politics

CONTENTS

Page ix
For the Reader

Page 1
A Knot in My Stomach

Page 22
Growing Up in the Other America

Page 44
From Camelot to the Inquisition

Page 77
A Greenhorn, A Professor

Page 103
The Circus Begins

Page 126
Are You a Beaner?

Page 154
The Politics of Politics

Page 178
Debatable Debates

Page 202
Threats, Tallies, Freedom

Page 223
Afterthought

GIVING GRACIAS

These pages are dedicated to the memory of my mother Angela Pulvirenti for drawing my dreams with her eyes in her homeland of Argentina and in her adopted land of Chile. They also are dedicated to John and our children, Jonathan and Christi, for their unconditional love and for allowing me to share my life with so many unpopular causes.

I also dedicate this book to my friends Nancy Fennel and Allison Adams for saving my body from the dark and bringing me back to life at the hospital in Los Angeles in 1997.

To a wonderful woman, Pat Lundval, for her constant advice and true friendship in the hardest moments, and to my friend of a lifetime, Pamela Driggs, for years of sisterhood.

Muchas gracias to my Latina friends who fight the battle with me day after day on our way to empowering the Latinos in our state.

This book developed from a simple journal with the help of many friends and colleagues. Their help was invaluable in re-writing, editing and correcting the final pages of the manuscript. The list is long and my appreciation goes to every one of them, but especially to Dr. Anne Beck, Richard Schaaf and Michael Sion.

I would also like to thank the many great women political leaders, elected officials and activists in northern Nevada who have opened the difficult roads for all of us and have been our guides on the long journey. The list of people is too long to mention everyone here, but among them are Jan Evans, Jean Ford, Maya Miller, Frankie Sue Del Papa, Sue Wagner, Bernice Mathews, Diana Glomb, Sheila Leslie, Virginia Cain and Jill Winter, to name just a few. To all of you I am extremely grateful, and I only hope that in years to come this list will include hundreds of Latina elected officials and political activists who will permanently open the doors to a better future.

I want the following pages to be a special tribute to the people who helped me during my difficult campaign and the voters who supported me on election day, 1994.

To all of you — mi eterna gratitud.

FOR THE READER

When I first decided to run for the Nevada Senate, I had no thought of writing a book about it. However, the experience of running for public office turned out to be so overwhelming that I began to keep a diary, a chronicle of my political campaign. I made entries almost every night for the duration of my campaign so as to safekeep my thoughts and feelings of the events.

The idea to write this book chronicling my campaign experiences slowly formed during my run for office. At first, I wanted to write the book in Spanish and publish it in another country, where it would shed light on the life of an immigrant, a Latina, who had ventured into the world of politics in the United States.

Near the end of the campaign, after losing any illusions I harbored about the fairness of the political process, I decided to publish the book in an English edition. I felt the need to provide a truthful account of what it was like for a Latina to run a political campaign in the U.S. in the '90s, and, in particular, in Nevada.

With the passage of time, the book broadened in scope to include a chronicle of my personal and political development in South America, my active support of Salvador Allende's bid for the presidency of Chile and my decision to emigrate from Chile in the aftermath of the brutal blow dealt the democratic ideals of the Allende administration.

It is my hope that this book serves Latinos and Latino communities to empower themselves. It is also my hope that these pages offer the American public a clear vision of the harsh realities of running a campaign for public office. Electoral politics in the U.S. is more of a game, a money game, than most of us want to admit. Generally speaking, the candidate who raises the most money is more than likely guaranteed victory. Most of your time is spent raising money, and little time, indeed, is spent establishing a meaningful dialog with citizens to ascertain and discuss *their* real concerns and needs. In short, running for public office today has little to do with real communication and education.

I do not want to be viewed as a victim, but rather as a survivor and passionate fighter. I am a concerned and engaged citizen committed to helping bring about needed change that will better the lives of the people of Nevada. Also, I feel deeply humbled, and proud, that 6,000 citizens shared my vision of Reno's future at the ballot box. For this base of support, I will always be thankful.

What follows is a personal account of a small political race in a small state, a detailed journal of how a campaign for public office in the U.S. is run as we approach the end of the century and the beginning of a new millennium. It is also the testimony of a Latina infused with a deep love for her new land and a profound sense of gratitude for the opportunities given her.

—Emma Sepúlveda

To my friend Reynaldo Martínez
for building bridges not walls

A Knot in My Stomach

"TRISHA, WHAT DO YOU think about me running for political office?"

Funny how one question can set in motion events that will envelop you like a cloak for months to come.

It was a rain-drenched February night. I was in a Japanese restaurant, Kyoto, not far from our house with my husband and some close friends. The restaurant is a small, family-run eatery with a dim interior and intimate ambiance. Because it makes the best sushi in town, it's a popular place for our group of friends.

It was in the restaurant's familiar but foreign confines, the table lit by orange candle glow, that I made my leap into American politics.

"Trisha, what do you think about me running for office?"

I trusted Trisha to give me an objective opinion. She had lobbied at the Nevada Legislature, and knew many of the major players in Nevada politics, including something of my political background and aspirations.

Trisha and her husband Paul had met my father, Hugo, a businessman who had run for office in Chile and later been appointed to a municipal post under Gen. Augusto Pinochet, the strongman who then ruled Chile. From what they could understand of the political conversations between my father and me, they had been shocked by how right-wing my father was. They knew that I, his daughter, was that dirty word, a liberal, and wondered how we had ever gotten along.

As Trisha and her husband knew, years earlier I had played with the idea of running for the County Commission. I had sat on many committees and community task forces for the Latino population and the community at large. I had also started a program for my Spanish students at the University of Nevada to use their language skills as volunteer translators and interpreters for immigrants, and that gave me an insight into the desperate needs of the people in my community. Because of this insight, I had a strong urge to roll up my sleeves and try to accomplish goals at the political level. Like many veterans of long hours of citizen activism, I felt frustrated at the pace of change. I believed I could make a real difference if only I could be a voice for these voiceless people. However, I also knew that it would be a tough race for the County Commission. I had decided at that time to wait a few years.

"Which office did you have in mind?" she asked.

I replied, "I was thinking of a run for the state Senate."

Trisha pondered. "I think you could do it, Emma," she said. "The only problem would be to raise the money. And money is everything in a political campaign. If you don't have the connections. . ."

"Well, I think I can run a campaign with very little money," I said perhaps too quickly. My idea has always been to run a grassroots campaign."

I'll always remember those heady first moments, sitting around the table with my husband and friends, the excitement breaking out.

"Do you really want to do this?" Trisha asked. "Jonathan is only six years old. He needs your time and attention. Do you know what you're getting yourself into? This is the nineties, Emma. Political campaigns are a dirty business. They're going to pry into your past to dig up whatever skeletons they can. And if they don't find them, they will make them up. You can forget about having a peaceful or private life from this point on."

It seems on that night I did not have ears to listen to warnings of the dangers of political campaigns in this country. I was focusing on the possibility of the wonderful things I could accomplish for so many people.

"You know," I said, "I have been very unhappy with the senator representing our district. That is someone I would love to take on."

A picture came to my mind of a man I had met several years before. It was at a barbecue, in a southwest Reno home. It had begun to rain. We all got wet from the sudden storm, but tried to maintain our good humor. However, among the laughs and the jokes, I heard a man say, "My $1,500 shoes are going to get ruined! How can you plan a barbecue and not prepare for this type of weather?"

I smiled and asked a friend, "Who's the Imelda Marcos clone?"

"That's our state senator," she said, "believe it or not."

From then on, whenever I encountered this man at social gatherings, I would observe him, trying not to stare. He always struck me as unreal. He seemed to be a person who could never fit in, always out of place, always uncomfortable with himself. Curious about this character, I began to read up on him.

It seems my senator had worked very little for a living because of a sizable inheritance. He had spent his twenties racing cars, working out, dating gorgeous women and getting a degree in education. Then he decided to enter politics, financed by his own large bank account. On his second try, he was elected to the state Senate as a Democrat supported by the labor unions, a man of the people and probably my type of candidate, someone I could have voted for. But he was a man who blew with the political winds. Prior to the end of his four-year term, he cut his hair, discarded the love beads around his neck, put on a three-piece Italian-made suit, and crossed party lines to become a Republican, declaring that the Democrats were out of touch with Ronald Reagan's America.

Now I was going to try to knock this man from his Senate seat. It seemed almost like a movie script.

I needed to know if my view of him as a vulnerable candidate was shared by my friends. Trisha knew the senator personally.

"I think he has some vulnerable spots," Trisha said. "Obviously, like every politician, he's made some mistakes. Also, did you know he lives in Las Vegas now?"

Las Vegas is a nine-hour drive from Reno, toward the southern end of the state. The vast geographic separation between Nevada's two major cities is a source of political friction, and has created a north-south schism in the Legislature. The rumor was that my state senator didn't live in a house in Reno anymore, but rented a small apartment here while his primary residence was in Las Vegas with his second wife and her son. It seemed he didn't live in the district he represented.

"He's not a very popular person," Trisha said. "He's disliked by many people because he is an egomaniac who is a pain to work with. He is obnoxious, the kind of politician everybody hates. You might get a lot of votes from people who dislike him even if they do not necessarily support you. On the other hand, many people will be afraid to support you, because he is vindictive. I have heard other people talk about the profile of a candidate who could take him on. It would be a female candidate who is more personable and more sensitive than he, and who is educated and a professional."

Trisha looked at me. "You know that you, too, have some shortcomings as a political candidate, she said." I was curious to know what she meant.

"Your biggest liability is that you were not born in this country and you have an accent."

At that moment, I didn't really take her comments seriously. This is a country of immigrants. Many people are foreign-born and have accents. Kissinger has an accent, right? Not that I'm a Kissinger, but the last thing that should matter in this country is where a person was born. I am a citizen of the United States of America. I had lived in Reno for over twenty years, more than the current senator. Surely, if that became an issue, I would win.

Trisha suggested that I should get opinions from some other people about my political aspirations.

"I know Howard Jones, a lobbyist whom I consider a real insider when it comes to the Assembly and the Senate," she said. "He's not in town but I'll get hold of him wherever he is, and have him call you."

"Really, tonight? It's already nine o'clock."

"He'll call you."

From that moment on I felt a knot in my stomach that did not loosen its grip until election night in November. We stayed through dessert at the restaurant, hashing over this dream that was strangely taking shape. It was all surreal. Our table was positioned near the center of the floor, and familiar faces passed by repeatedly in greeting. I intended that our table's conversation remain private. Deciding to run for office, after all, is an extremely personal issue; it is only after the public announcement that your privacy is utterly shredded and you become fair game, to be scrutinized by anyone and everyone.

It so happened that our friend's parents were dining at a nearby table. Trisha's mother came up to us as they were leaving. Immediately, everyone at the table started announcing my plans to the world. "Emma's thinking about running for office. What do you think?"

Another couple we knew stopped by our table. "Emma has some news to tell you," John said.

"No, I don't!" I blurted with a weak smile, feeling insecure and confused.

"Are you pregnant?" they asked.

That night after I read a story to my son, I went to my office and I started to read again Isabel Allende's *Paula*. The knot still gripped my stomach. I watched the 11 o'clock news and *Nightline*, then read some more. I felt a bit foolish waiting up for the lobbyist. He was never going to call.

I consoled myself with the knowledge I was hardly a political candidate yet. I could still back out. What had I done — expressed an interest in running to a couple friends? I could always tell them it wasn't the right time in my life. I could always reconsider.

At 12:30 a.m., the phone rang.

It was Howard Jones. I could hardly make out his voice.

"I'm in Vegas," he said. "I can't believe what I heard."

"Really?" I stammered.

"I talked to Trisha," he said. "I'm meeting here with some people from the Democratic party who are looking for a candidate that could run against the senator in District 4."

It became one of the strangest phone conversations I've ever had. I found myself pouring my heart out to this man, telling him what I wanted to accomplish in politics, my feelings, my dreams, and I had no idea who he was, other than he was a lobbyist (and a Republican at that!)

I was getting my first taste of the drug of politics — the rush of an adrenaline high. Someone had called me about the race. I was hungry for assurance. Could the senator be defeated? Could I raise the money to wage a serious campaign? Could someone like me — immigrant, brown-skinned with an accent, female, liberal persuasion and all — hope to compete with a conservative, wealthy, white male in Nevada?

"Yes, indeed, I think he is vulnerable, because he lives in Vegas and everybody knows that," he said. "You're right, he hasn't pushed anything meaningful through the Legislature since he helped create the Consumer Advocate's Office during his first term, when he was a Democrat. However, don't forget he was constantly in the newspaper during the last legislative session when they were trying to reform SIIS [The Nevada State Industrial Insurance System]. The average reader only knows that he supposedly saved the state millions of dollars by redesigning SIIS. They do not know the truth, that his work on SIIS was designed to protect the casinos, to the detriment of the workers. Other than that, there's nothing really crucial that he has done."

I asked him about what Trisha had said about my own political vulnerability. He didn't answer my question about whether my ethnicity would prove a campaign liability.

"Let's talk about other things," he said.

I couldn't sleep at all that night. I tried to return to my reading of Isabel Allende's book, but I could not read anymore. I wished, as my ancestors had done in moments of indecision and doubt, that I could consult the spirits to guide me onto the right path. I went downstairs and leafed through some of my father's political brochures. Almost a year before, he'd run for mayor in La Florida, a suburb of Santiago, Chile. He lost. It was an exhausting campaign. Afterward, he became very ill. His back hurt. He thought he was just tired.

One day, he collapsed. They ran tests at the hospital and found he had bone cancer. Six months later, he died. His sudden death made him a hero. He didn't get enough votes to win the election, but his funeral attracted the biggest crowd in the town's history. He gathered together the people he needed to win the election, but only when it was too late for them to vote for him.

That night I read through my father's campaign literature. He painted himself, with much satisfaction, as a conservative. He was for cutting taxes and granting breaks to big business. I stared at a campaign picture he had sent me. I disliked the photo even though he had mailed it with so much pride. He was seated with key players in Chile, including Gen. Augusto Pinochet, the man I have perhaps feared and hated most in my life.

We had our differences, father and I. I was the black sheep of the family in many ways. He had wanted me to be a physician; I wanted to be a professor. He had wanted me to remain in Chile; I had chosen a life in the United States. He was a political conservative; I was a liberal.

But that night, I felt very close to him. At least we shared the will to win at politics, to shape society. He had campaigned in his native Chile, and I was now campaigning in a faraway land that I loved deeply and had adopted for all the best reasons. Dad always thought one of the best ways to change the world was through politics. How I wished my father were alive right then. He would have been the first person I would have called. I would have asked him what he thought. I think he would have said, "Go for it."

The other person I thought of during that long, sleepless night was my mother. She had lived almost her entire life as a foreigner. She was the daughter of a wealthy Italian immigrant in Argentina. After marrying my father, she moved to Chile, but never changed her Argentinean citizenship. She knew what it meant to be forever a foreigner in someone else's land. She would have told me not to run for office.

Although my mother always told me that there was no limit to what I could accomplish, she was very afraid of women jumping into an activity that was traditionally off-limits to them — especially politics. For her, it was a man's game.

Unfortunately, both my parents were gone. I felt lonely and sad, and not knowing whom to turn to, I began to cry. It was four o'clock in the morning.

I went to sleep with the knot in my stomach, my eyes red from crying, and the vision of Chile and my parents in my dreams.

The next few days I felt like I was leading a double life. I was a Spanish literature professor at the university during the day and the remainder of the time an insecure immigrant woman who was thinking about making a run for political office.

It was best that I didn't share my doubts or my ideas with anyone. I needed to learn more about the issues and what it meant to become involved in northern Nevada politics. I didn't want the entire affair to snowball to the point where others were making the decision for me about running for public office.

News of my interest in the senate race had quickly filtered through the state Democratic Party. The Republican lobbyist, Howard Jones, to whom I had spoken also had spoken to Democrats in Las Vegas, and the news of my consideration reached Northern Nevada Assemblywoman, Jan Evans, who had been one of the first persons I'd met when I arrived in Reno twenty years earlier. She was someone I had always respected and admired.

"I heard through the grapevine that you are thinking about joining us," she said on the phone. "We sure need people like you, Emma. I don't think there's a lot of representation from minorities. I want to make myself clear that I'm not asking you to be a token, but I definitely think our party and the Legislature needs someone like you."

We covered my stands on basic issues such as abortion (I'm pro-choice) and term limits (I'm for them). She also bestowed upon me four pieces of advice, to be used if I decided to run. First, always neutralize your enemies by working with them and talking to them. Second, go up the political ladder but do not forget to look back and give your hand to other women coming up behind you. Third, trust yourself and your instincts, more than other people's advice. Fourth, always look to your true support: your family and good friends.

After our initial conversation, Jan called almost daily. Then she invited me to breakfast with another female senator from northern Nevada, Diane Glomb. Jan said that the senator wanted to talk to me. It seemed that some of the Democratic party regulars wanted to recruit me, but I was so scared that I felt suspicious rather than flattered. What if they wanted me to jump into a race in which I had no chance? Who was the one who was going to get burned and perhaps kill her political future forever if she made the wrong choice about running now?

My only real confidante was my husband, John. He reiterated that it was our decision and no one else's business. He was as politically naive as I was.

A week later, I agreed to meet with my friend, Jan, and Senator Glomb. As they had requested, we met at a place where no one would recognize us. I was concerned that this was really a spy mission. I could not figure out why these people were seemingly so paranoid about a simple political race.

We met at the Airport Plaza Hotel at seven a.m. I arrived early, nervous as hell. Senator Glomb said she was very excited for me. She also told me not to be concerned about being a political outsider.

"Listen, I was an outsider," she said. " But I was very visible in the pro-choice movement. One day, the party asked me to run for the Senate." She had defeated a conservative, male Republican. It was not an easy feat in Nevada.

As it turned out, she had decided not to seek re-election. Supposedly, the Republican Senate Majority Leader, Bill Raggio, possibly the most powerful politician in Nevada, had targeted her Senate seat for Republican control. That meant a large, well-financed effort would be directed at reclaiming her seat for the GOP. The Republicans held a slim 11-10 majority in the Senate and were fearful of losing the edge. So the only female senator in Northern Nevada had become a marked woman. She had chosen not to fight another mean-spirited battle. She explained why.

"From now on, you have to know, Emma, that your life is going to be very difficult. They did terrible things to me to try to stop me from running that first time. And after I was elected, it was nearly impossible for me to find a job. Other personal tragedies happened. Your family is going to take a lot of abuse, and your relationship with your husband is going to be tested."

If I had been worried about getting a snow job to get me to run for office, this surely wasn't it. This pair was painting a bleak picture. One thing in particular stuck with me. It was something that my friend Jan had said, and which I couldn't make much sense of at the time. She said, "Emma, you are going to start getting phone calls from people asking you not to run. This is a chapter from the Political Intimidation textbook. They are going to harass you. They are going to try to get your friends to talk you out of running. You'll have trouble even finding someone to run your campaign."

I laughed. Come on! This is Reno. No one even knew me yet. What's more, I was running for a state Senate seat, not some high-powered national office. Her description of the political landscape sounded more like the Sicily my grandfather had left, rather than Reno, the Biggest Little City in the World.

"Emma, listen to me," she said with a straight face. "Don't go out alone. Don't become unraveled if people start talking about you to your students at the university. Don't trust anyone. Believe it or not, this is what it means to run for political office in the nineties."

As I got in my car, I thought, "I admire Jan. She's a neat

lady. But I think she's losing it."

As it turned out, it was as if I had spoken to an *adivina*, a fortune teller, in some tiny village in South America, who had read my tea leaves and told me my future.

Everything she told me that morning was to come true.

The next week, a Las Vegas senator flew up to Reno to meet with me. It was late April, and the filing deadline was in June. He told me I needed to file the next day. He reassured me that I shouldn't worry about campaign funds because *he* would raise all the money I needed.

I refused his offer since I saw him as a salesman trying to close an unacceptable deal. There was something too good to be true about the whole interaction. I decided to develop my own organization. Later events proved that my instincts about this "snow job" were true: the senator who had promised me the moon never raised a single dollar in campaign contributions for me.

Soon after I rejected his "deal," the Democratic Senate minority leader, Dina Titus, flew up from Las Vegas. She asked to meet in a place where no one would recognize us. By now I was getting used to this "aside" game. We decided to meet at a local pie shop on South Virginia Street in Reno. It was four in the afternoon; the place was dead.

She was very cool to me at first, feeling me out. She was intelligent, very witty and had a great deal of political savvy. A politician who holds her own; who doesn't fool around. After a full hour of interrogating me about my views, stands, and intentions, she suddenly broke into a large smile. "You know, a lot of people have called to tell me about you," she said. "But I like you much more now that I have met you and talked with you." So we talked about my issues for the next two hours. She was satisfied I was a serious and conscientious candidate for office.

I knew the pieces were falling into place for me to wage a serious campaign.

I soon caught wind of a letter. It was signed by the executive director of the Greater Reno-Sparks Chamber of Commerce. The letter was directed to presiden Angeles Ortega, of the local Hispanic Business Council, a division of the chamber, of which I was a member. The letter from the chamber started, "We are reminding you that you must refrain completely from political issues and from endorsing or recruiting candidates. . ." In the next section of the letter, the executive director identified the source of the complaint. "At the same time, our state senator in District 4 has contacted us [the chamber] to let us know that you [the president of the Hispanic Council] are endorsing and supporting a candidate to run against him. This is in violation of chamber rules. . ." The letter closed with a warning that sanctions were possible and could result in the Hispanic Business Council losing its affiliation and non-profit status.

The president of the Hispanic Council called me immediately. She was extremely upset. She confided, "You know, they are accusing us of endorsing you and supporting you. Personally, I had no idea you were definitely going to run for the Senate."

I was shocked at the letter. I offered to call the press immediately and say that although I was a member of the group, there was no connection between the Hispanic Business Council and my campaign. She preferred an immediate meeting with the chamber officers to assure them that the Hispanic Business Council had not recruited me or endorsed my campaign.

Of course, the rumors circulated to the chamber of commerce had no basis in fact. It appeared that the current District 4 senator and his friends were attempting to neutralize my potential supporters by intimidating my contact groups. He was effectively instilling fear in anyone who might consider helping me.

They also used other tactics.

I was a member of a committee for a student's master's of arts examination in foreign languages. The student called me a few days before his examination was scheduled to be held. He told me that a certain assemblyman had just phoned him to say that he should advise me against running for office. The student reported that the assemblymen had advised against my running for office because "it was going to cost me." And "there are going to be problems for her [me] in the future. No one will give her a penny, and she's going to make a fool of herself."

This unlucky student was confronted with this dilemma two days before he was to take his exam. He was distraught. He didn't know whether to tell me about the call and ruin my objectivity in judging his test performance, or to keep the information to himself and risk news of the call reaching me anyway, making it even worse for him.

I was so thankful that he was able to tell me about the call. I reassured him that everything would be okay. I saw the position in which I had been so skillfully placed by my opponents. If the questions I composed for his examination were too easy, the student might feel that I went easy on him because I didn't want to make political waves. If the questions were too hard, he might believe that I tried to fail him because he had told me about the threatening phone call. To avoid further conflicts or recriminations, I removed myself from the student's committee. Although we don't have baseball in Chile, I was quickly learning the meaning of "hardball."

Then, not long after these incidents, the phone calls at home and at the office started.

The callers were anonymous males and females. "Are you the crazy lady who wants to run for the Senate? You don't have a chance!" *Click.*

The calls escalated. They grew disgustingly obscene.

"You're the dumb fuck that wants to get into politics? You don't belong in this community. Goddamn foreigners, first you ruin this country and now you want to run our lives."

At first, John and I tried to zero in on the culprits. We would lie awake at night trying to figure out who they could be, whose voice did it sound like? Whenever the telephone rang we would run to answer, afraid that our six-year-old son would pick up the telephone before we did and hear some obscene message. Then, little by little, we realized that the whole town knew I intended to run for the Senate. There were no more secrets. We finally gave up trying to figure out who these twisted individuals were.

To fuel the fire, a Las Vegas-based newspaperman, John Ralston, devoted his weekly political column to my entering the race. Papers in Las Vegas and Reno printed his column. It began:

> *It is likely to be the most expensive, most divisive and most vitriolic legislative contest in Northern Nevada history.*
>
> *It will inflame sectional passions, cause inter-party disruptions and engender skittishness within the lobbying corps. . . .*
>
> *The race in question pits a three-term GOP senator, a marquee player in last session's State Industrial Insurance System reform fight and the Majority Leader's reliable lieutenant, against newcomer Emma Sepúlveda, a Chilean-born, University of Nevada foreign language professor, active in the Hispanic community and with plenty of volunteers ready to walk precincts.*

The column's unverified assumption was that the Democratic Minority Leader, Dina Titus, wanted to drain Republican coffers by forcing the Republican senator in District 4 into an expensive campaign, thus clearing the way for other Democrats to defeat Republicans around the state, tilt the Senate majority toward the Democratic party, and land the Minority Leader in the plush office of the Republican Senate Majority Leader, Bill Raggio.

The column gave me even more questions to ponder during my already sleepless nights. Most of all, I asked myself over and over if I had the emotional and physical strength to enter the "most expensive, most divisive and most vitriolic race in Northern Nevada history." The knot in my stomach seemed to be saying maybe I wasn't ready to be the first Latina women in the state Senate.

After this additional publicity, the crank telephone calls increased. Our phone number has always been unlisted, but that posed no barrier for some of the "true believers" in the general public. They began telephoning me at my university office as well. I'd try to keep them on the line. "Who are you? Why are you doing this?" They'd say, "Oh, you know damn well." Then they'd hang up.

John and I figured they were just trying to irritate me and in time the calls would stop. I believed that they were people who were hoping that I would panic and not file. However, one Friday morning, as John and I were ready to leave for work, the phone rang. I was standing in the kitchen. My son, Jonathan, was walking out to his father's car and stopped in the doorway when the phone rang.

I picked up the phone. A man with a deep voice that I recognized from previous calls said, "You know, we're going to kill you if you insist on doing this. Don't take this as bullshit that isn't real."

Jonathan sensed something was wrong. He looked at me with fear in his eyes. As usual after the phone calls, I smiled as if nothing was wrong so he wouldn't be afraid. I felt that my face was probably as white as it is ever going to get.

Then three of us went outside and got in the car. We dropped our son off at school without a word. Then I faced John. "That was a really bad phone call. Now they say they're going to hurt me."

He slammed his fist on the steering wheel. He said he was going to drive to a store and buy a Caller ID device.

John drove me to work. Along the way, I felt the same fear I had experienced in Chile during the military takeover. I was sad, but mostly scared. My whole body was shaking and my mouth achingly dry with the fear that seemed to be taking control of my life again.

Around noon, John picked me up and we went home for lunch. Then I got in my car and he got in his truck. He said he was going back to work. A short time later, we ran into each other at Radio Shack in Park Lane, each trying to buy the same little Caller ID machine.

I picked up Jonathan at 3 p.m. from school. Perhaps because of what had occurred in the morning, he immediately ran into my bedroom when we got home. Before I could stop him, he hit the play-back on the answering machine.

I heard him scream.

"Mom, they're going to kill you," he said, after I'd rushed into the room.

I played back the message. It was a man's voice speaking again, this time explaining *how* was I going to be killed. There was a gagging, strangling sound. I tried to comfort my son by telling him that someone was just playing around. I suggested to him that it was a trick, a song maybe. Six-year-olds aren't so easily fooled. Jonathan made the connection with the call that morning.

"That's what they're going to do to you, Mom," he said. I saw again the heartrending fear in his young eyes. Suddenly, I felt profoundly guilty and selfish for trying to pursue a political career that was causing my family so much pain.

That weekend, John went out of town to a golf tournament at the Carson Valley Inn, about 50 miles south. Because of the death threats, Cristina, my teen-age niece who lived with us, Jonathan, and I all slept in my bedroom. We were scared. When a call came that night, I was almost relieved. I was waiting for the call. Finally, we were going to catch these people!

The call sounded as if it came from a bar or a place where a party was going on. You could hear music and other voices in the background. Cristina dashed into the kitchen, where the Caller ID device was connected to the phone. For the first time, we discovered that the device could be blocked from receiving the caller's number. We realized we couldn't trace the calls, and later we also learned that the Caller ID device didn't work on tracking cellular phone numbers either. That night, we spent our time huddled together in my bed, unable to sleep.

The following Monday, I talked to a friend of mine in the Reno Police Department, Officer Carlos Madrid. I didn't want to make the calls public; I didn't want anyone to think I was exploiting the issue for publicity.

My friend tried to reassure me by confiding, "Basically, Emma, if they're going to kill you, they're not going to call you to let you know," he said. "Forget that, live your life. Try to trace the calls and call them right back and tell them off. Keep the telephone numbers and turn them into me. But don't panic, because that's what they want." With these semi-reassuring words, I returned home and tried to focus on my decision, putting the fear aside.

However, one more incident highlighted the difficulties I would encounter in my campaign.

The University of Nevada had awarded me its Thornton Peace Award, a yearly honor bestowed upon someone in the university community who has worked to achieve peace through non-violent means anywhere in the world. I was acknowledged for my work in Chile, helping the mothers of *los desaparecidos*, the people who had disappeared during the reign of terror under General Pinochet following the bloody military overthrow of President Salvador Allende in 1973.

The award was very special to me. It meant that somebody somewhere recognized my work, or anyone's work, in defense of human rights. Most importantly, the prize signaled that the women of Chile were recognized for their ceaseless struggle for justice.

At the ceremony's reception, a woman I have known for years, a wife of a retired English professor, was the first in the reception line to congratulate me. She is well known in Reno social circles. She approached me and gave me a big, disarming hug.

"I heard," she whispered softly, wine fumes on her breath, "that you are going to run for the Senate." She smiled.

"Well let me tell you, honey, you are a foreigner, how could you dare get involved in the politics of our country? You don't belong here. How would you like it if I went to your country and ran for political office? I'm going to tell you right now, we had a party last week, a woman's group, and you were the laughing stock of the party. You have a horrible accent. The first time that you give a speech, people are going to be rolling on the floor, laughing. It will be a miracle if you get 1,000 votes. And let me tell you, honey, I hear you're going to do this so-called door-to-door campaign. The only votes that you're going to get is if you wear a mini-skirt and the guy who opens the door gets horny and then votes for you."

At first, I couldn't say anything, I was so shocked and hurt that I thought I would cry. I fought back the tears. I felt violated. I could not believe that somebody I had worked with on so many projects, and who belonged to so many civic organizations, could be so coarse, callous, and an apparent racist. I felt humiliated that somebody with a slightly different skin color and a different place of birth would attack me in such a personal way. I left the ceremony without another word, my night of shared triumph with other women painfully ruined.

But it is ironic how blatant prejudice and racism can make you see the world so clearly. At home that night, I could not sleep again, but I finally came to a decision about the campaign. I knew then that I was going to run to be a voice for the people who have never been represented before and to demonstrate that immigrants who chose to belong to this country are as much a part of the fabric of the nation as those who are here by accident of birth. We, who have freely chosen this democratic life, have not only the right but the duty to be a voice in the political process.

That week I sent out press releases announcing my candidacy for the Democratic party candidate for the Senate, District 4. With my friends and political supporters gathered at my newly established campaign headquarters, John and I drove to the County Administration Complex. I paid my $100 filing fee at the registration office.

I was now an official candidate for Senate District 4, the first name on the Democratic ballot. I was officially in the race for the state Senate seat, District 4. That day I will always remember.

Upon my return to campaign headquarters, I gave my first official campaign speech. . . .

This is not only a really important day in the life of Emma Sepúlveda, my family and my friends, but it is an important day for my community.

Today, I have filed the paperwork to become a candidate for the 4th District of the Nevada State Senate.

I am doing this because I believe that our community needs an independent voice in the State Senate.

I did not arrive at this decision easily.

I was told by many people, even some friends, not to run.

I was told that I would be running against an entrenched incumbent who had all the power of his office to defeat me.

I was told that I could not raise the money.

I was told that my character would be attacked and it was made clear to my friends and supporters that they should not support me.

I was even told that my accent would result in losing support.

But, given the struggles I have faced throughout my life, these things just represent new challenges to me.

As the campaign proceeds, you will soon discover that I am not your typical candidate for public office.

I am not a polished and refined politician. I do not care about projecting an image. Rather, I am a person with deep convictions, perseverance, and commitment.

You will know where Emma Sepúlveda stands on the issues before and after the election.

You may be asking yourselves why am I running?

Well, I have spent all my life working passionately for a variety of causes and beliefs, some popular and some not so popular. But the one thing that has been consistent with all of these is that I have worked to give voice to the voiceless.

I know what it is to live in a dollar per hour and have no health insurance.

As an educator, I witness on a daily basis the struggles that our young people face in trying to succeed and achieve their goals.

But just as important as all of these things is the fact that I am the personification of the American Dream. I am the living and breathing proof that this dream exists and is alive.

This country and this community have given me wonderful opportunities to achieve success.

For this, I am grateful. It is because of these wonderful opportunities that I am committed to public service. I want to work to ensure that our future generations are given the same opportunities that were given to me.

Serving you in the State Senate is what I can do, at least in part, to repay my debt of gratitude.

There are a number of things that make Northern Nevada a great place to live. One is the tremendous diversity of people that live and work here. Consequently the Sepúlveda campaign will be about inclusion and not division.

However, while our community is a great place to live, it is faced with many problems. Our quality of life is threatened by rising incidents of violent crime. Our overcrowded classrooms and high dropout rates are threatening our ability to compete economically.

It would be dishonest for me to stand up here and tell you that I alone have the answer or the power to solve these problems.

These are community problems and therefore they require community solutions.

But, what I can promise you is that when I am elected, I will be an independent voice for our community. . .

The knot in my stomach remained with me the entire time I was delivering the speech.

Growing Up in the Other America

SYLVESTRE PULVIRENTI, my mother's father, was a giant of a man. He was born at the base of a volcano, in the little Sicilian town abutting Mount Etna. It was fitting, because his Italian nature was given to powerful eruptions. He was a human mountain — a hulking 6-feet-9. His grand passions led him to immigrate to Argentina in the late-nineteenth century, during the great wave of European migration to South America that paralleled that of the great empire-building country in the northern half of the Western Hemisphere. There, in the rugged Argentine interior, Grandpa carved out for himself his own ranching empire.

Sylvestre was one of two sons. His father had been killed during warfare as a conscript in the Italian army. His brother died in a later conflict. And his mother, my maternal great-grandmother, resolved to send her remaining son to seek his fortune in a more promising world. She had already lost two men to war.

Sylvestre was twenty years old when he boarded a ship packed with fellow Italian dreamers to cross the Mediterranean and Atlantic. He wrote copious poems along the way. The feeling among his generation was that the New World promised untold riches for those who would make the voyage and build up a stake to buy a farm. It was said the governments of the young South American nations were practically giving land away. Sylvestre knew his only hope to escape Sicily's poverty lay in this virgin continent. He believed implicitly that his dream and his voyage would totally transform his existence.

And so it did.

He landed at the port of Buenos Aires, where a sizable community of his countrymen was already established. The wide-eyed, strapping youth tagged along with a group of his ship-mates who had relatives in the city. He soon landed a job in a small *finca*, a farm, as a laborer. Day after day, week after week, Sylvestre stubbornly squirreled his wages away under his mattress, distrusting banks. He made few efforts to learn the language of the New World, Spanish. Throughout his life, Grandpa always held himself above Argentineans. He saw himself as a European, different from and better than the Argentineans. He couldn't digest the culture of the population of his adopted land. Their looks, their ways, were foreign and, thus, inferior.

Although he lacked language and cultural skills, the newcomer quickly absorbed the farming knowledge of his new environment. He learned about machinery, weather patterns and cultivation techniques. Within a year of his arrival, he had moved to Mendoza in the southwestern wine country in the shadow of the Andes. There, he found San Rafael, a tiny town outside the city that had very inexpensive acreage for sale. The catch was that the climate was crazy. There were *las piedras* — gigantic hailstones that could demolish an entire crop in a single storm. There were also periodic attacks by swarms of *las langostas* — locusts that would descend in a cloud and voraciously devour grapevines until only the wire stands were left.

Grandpa obstinately took his chances anyway. This was just the sort of challenge for a man like him. And so he had his first farm: a small plot of land for cultivating grapes to sell to wine makers. He persevered and did well enough to sell the plot and buy a bigger parcel. That set the pattern. Grandpa began to buy up all the surrounding land. He grew wealthy. He began to produce his own wine on a small scale. In time, he married a Chilean woman, who died after giving birth to their fifth child. Even this didn't slow him down.

It wasn't until his late forties that his friends introduced this enormous and enormously successful Italian widower to a 19-year-old Argentinean woman of Spanish descent, whose name was Concepción.

Grandma was true to her name. She conceived for Grandpa

seven more children — five daughters and two sons. This pleased him from a practical standpoint. Farm work requires much labor. Not only did Grandpa hire workers, but all his children were made to till the land. Nor did his attitude discriminate. Grandpa didn't care if you were male or female. He needed extra hands and his kids were going to serve that purpose. Five daughters were as good as five sons.

My mother, Angela, was the first child born to Grandma. Although Angela grew up working in the fields, she still acquired a good education. Grandpa believed girls should go to school to learn reading and writing as well as master the essential feminine skills of cooking, sewing and embroidering. As a child, Angela walked miles every day to the bus stop to go to school. Years after she was grown, Grandpa donated the land to construct an elementary school in San Rafael.

Angela finished high school and intended to earn a degree as a crafts teacher, but a year before graduation Grandpa withdrew his support. For Grandpa, an education was essential to both sexes, but what Angela had learned was sufficient. He told her, "I send you to school to prepare yourself to be a good wife, not to go and earn a salary like a man." Angela could not argue the point with this man who controlled her entire existence.

The Argentina of that time was very traditional, macho, male-dominated, and a Catholic society. To this day, only Catholics can become president. This ground rule caused Carlos Menem, who is of Syrian extraction, to convert to Catholicism before qualifying for the highest office.

A nation's character can't help but influence the individuals and families that live in it. And so Argentina, its history and policies, shaped the destiny of my own family. Because of its vast natural resources and the surfeit of immigrants, Argentina began to view itself as the bright hope of the continent — the nation that would grow into an economic powerhouse and major player on the world stage. At times, she even seemed headed toward fulfilling this prophecy. Buenos Aires has ranked up with London and Paris as a center of fashion. The meat industry,

built up by the romantic exploits of the wild-spirited *gauchos* —
the cowboys of the pampas — created an economic boom for
the nation.

But the curse of Latin America is not so easily overcome.
Argentina's Achilles heel has been the same bane that has plagued
the rest of the continent — political instability. For much of the
19th Century, power was concentrated in the hands of the few
— the wealthy landowners. It was they who controlled the elections. Yet this was to change not long after the new century
dawned.

In 1916, Hipolito Irigoyen came to power, aided by election
reform and buoyed by consistent economic prosperity. The
miracle of a democratic giant in South America appeared to many
to have become realized. Indeed, Argentina maintained a surprisingly liberal government until 1929, when the Great Depres-
sion disrupted the world economy. The next year, the
Argentinean military took over control of the government, and
has never really let go, despite frequent power struggles between
civilians and military elites. Military leaders have either ruled
Argentina directly or been the power behind the scenes ever
since.

The first joke about Argentina I heard in Chile, was that
Argentina was like a long-playing record: It had 33 revolutions
per minute. Yet, none of these changes seemed to affect Grandpa's
immutable world view in which he was king.

Grandpa was an intellectual, well-versed in literature and
philosophy; but he was never a great socializer. He held himself
apart from Argentineans. He thought of himself more as an ex-
patriate than an immigrant. Grandpa had a dissonant accent when
he spoke Spanish, and there were certain words for which our
family always used the Italian. Grandpa and Grandma were always *nono* and *nona*, not *abuelo* and *abuela*, to us.

But even Sylvestre Pulvirenti could not block Angela, so
much like her father, from following her spirit that blew as freely
as the wind.

Indeed, a gale was kicking up just beyond Grandpa's world;

it was ready to blow in from the west.

José Hugo Sepúlveda was a fair-skinned young man of Spanish descent. He was an adventurer from Chile. Hugo, the name he went by, attended a private Catholic university in Santiago, the Chilean capital. There he studied chemistry. His father owned land in southern Chile and Hugo had become an experienced *huaso*, the Chilean equivalent of the *gaucho*.

Taking the summers off from his chemistry studies, Hugo hired himself out for the dangerous and arduous mission of leading livestock over a secret pass through the Andes, from Chile into Argentina. To do so was an illegal bypassing of customs and duties, but the work was available. Young, rugged *huasos* were in great demand. They were the ones who could cope with inclement weather and high altitudes on horseback while leading cattle on a month-long trek through the mountains, all the time avoiding border checkpoints. This suited Hugo's rambunctious spirit.

One summer, Hugo ended up in San Rafael. He delivered his herd to the landlords and received his payment. That weekend, Angela was representing her father at the inaugural ceremony for the new elementary school for which he had donated the land. Angela was sitting next to her mother, Concepcion, at this affair when an irresistibly handsome and polite young cowboy introduced himself to the mother. Although she didn't know it, he had crashed the dance party. Hugo asked the older woman for permission to dance with her daughter.

At the moment the two young people began to dance a beautiful tango, Angela knew that this was the man of her life, as she reminded me over and over again when I was a child being put to bed. At the end of the evening, Hugo explained he had to return to Chile to resume college. He told her he was only in the business of bringing animals over the pass during summer. Of course, he never did add that it was all illegal.

Back in Chile, Hugo began writing Angela love letters that she kept for nearly forty years until her death in 1985. After a year of correspondence, Hugo asked Angela to marry him. He intended to drop out of college and move to Argentina. He also wrote to her parents — and Grandpa Sylvestre erupted. He could not accept that his daughter — his favorite daughter at that!— would marry a foreigner, much less a college dropout with no money. Grandpa implored Angela not to marry this Hugo. And he made it very clear: should she flout him and marry, he would not give her away or attend her wedding.

She said that was fine with her. And so the first of Sylvestre Pulvirenti's children by his second wife was betrothed without his consent, support or presence. Hugo and Angela married in a small church in San Rafael. The fabric of her gown was ordered from Buenos Aires; the trappings were the finest. Dad's family and friends arrived from Chile. The knot was tied.

A large, festive party followed the wedding ceremony, and took place in Grandpa's vineyard. Sylvestre had reasoned that while he had refused to attend the wedding, whatever was done was done. He knew that she was still his daughter, defiant though she was. The reception that Sylvestre hosted was boisterous, Italian-style, with festive accordions and nonstop dancing. Grandpa danced the first dance with his daughter.

Mom and Dad began married life in the town of San Juan, not far from Mendoza. Dad, now an immigrant to Argentina, had gotten a job at a hydroelectric plant and had also arranged for his new wife to work washing the clothes of the factory employees. For Angela, this job was an excruciating humiliation for an educated woman from a wealthy family. In her diary, Mom recorded that the indignity of the menial labor reminded her of her father's warnings that Hugo was a real loser.

But Dad was not a loser. He was very hard-working, a typically resourceful immigrant who found successful ways to support his family. After Mom got pregnant, they moved to Mendoza and rented a modest home with a warehouse in back, where Dad designed and built batteries. He'd purchase what parts he needed, and from this humble start, he developed a prosperous business.

My sister, Ana María, was the first-born child, in 1948, and I was born in 1950. It was a tumultuous period for Argentina. I have always felt that my destiny was shaped by the political atmosphere of the countries in which I have lived. While military rule persisted in Argentina from 1930, chaos was always close by. Then in 1946, Col. Juan Perón became president. Perón started his political career as labor minister. He strengthened the unions and supported higher wages, and when he became president — carried into office by the unions — he granted immense powers to the work force. His bigger supporter were the *descamisados*, people who constituted the backbone of the nation's labor.

Grandpa hated Peron. Grandpa, of course, was a classic conservative. He saw Perón as giving far too much power to the working class and changing too many practices. In the beginning, Col. Perón seemed to foster stability in Argentina. But people like Grandpa saw nothing but doom ahead. To Grandpa, Argentina was going to become a country run by losers. He saw Perón as a vile political opportunist married to an uneducated woman from a poor background, both hell-bent on sticking it to the upper class. I grew up hearing that Perón was an evil person and Evita, his wife, was a whore. I didn't even know, of course, what a whore was. But I kept hearing the word *puta* around my house.

Perón, in reality, was a staunch nationalist who discouraged foreign investment. Argentina, he said, could finally rise to world power by becoming self-sufficient. This she could achieve only by developing manufacturing and exports. Evita became her husband's chief assistant. For a brief period, it was a golden era: the Argentinean version of Camelot.

I remember as a small child looking through Ana María's story books from school. One of my favorite tales was titled, "Santa Evita," about Eva Perón. My sister sang a song by the same name. Years later, when I went to the Broadway show, "Evita," and heard the music, I was carried back to that idyllic time. Later in my life, I read much about Evita and came to admire her courage. She never forgot her humble origins, though it would have been convenient for her once she had married Col. Perón. As the first lady, she always reached out to the poor. She opened schools for orphans and initiated massive vaccination programs for children. She became the compassionate face of her husband's administration.

Even though my mother was never a supporter of Eva Peron, I could hear my mother's voice in the words of the song, "Don't cry for me Argentina, the truth is I never left you . . ." My mother's soul always remained in Argentina.

Of course, stability in Latin America is normally the stillness before the storm. Evita died of cancer in 1952. The tempest arrived for her husband in 1955. Perón's tide of relentless reforms had begun to create a backlash. In time, a towering wave came crashing down and Perón lost the backing of his main supporters — the unions. Then the Catholic Church withdrew its support. Soon, political unrest consumed the country and even reached our remote rural region.

In Mendoza, a group of people set fire to a church near our house. Mom blamed the Perónistas. As we watched firemen battling the blaze, she told us, "You see, this is what Peronistas will do. They will kill the church, burn saints." Mom was a devout Catholic. This was the last attack she could tolerate. Without my sister or I knowing it, Mom and Dad began planning to leave Argentina.

Ana María and I were aware that something momentous was suddenly afoot in our land. As Perón lost his grip on power, we'd turn on the radio and hear martial music followed by an authoritarian voice announcing, "The order of the day is . . ." The government was trying to mobilize workers to go out into the streets in demonstrations of support.

"Oh, these Peronistas!" Mom would say. "They're going to destroy us!" I still wasn't even certain what a Peronista was. Public demonstrations and confrontations had become routine by now.

A medical student, Coco, who lived around the corner and was a close friend of the family, was against Perón. He would come over to our place very excited after a clash, saying, "We fought them, and we're going to win. We're going to take them out of power." He'd tell my sister about massive student protests, about how the Peronistas would show up to confront them, then soldiers would crash into the Peronistas. Sometimes, he said, such a melee would follow that no one knew whom they were shooting at. Though I was a little girl, I could sense I was living in a place that was out of control. I could not understand why people were so happy to see their countrymen beaten or killed.

By now, Dad had a thriving, middle-sized factory. It, too, was not immune to the troubles. Sometimes his workers wouldn't show up. Dad worried he wasn't moving his products as he needed to. What had seemed such a bright future a few short years before now appeared utterly uncertain.

One night, I heard Mom weeping in another room, saying, "What are we going to do? Maybe we should go live with my parents," and Dad saying, "I think I should go back to Chile, and send for you later."

National discord eventually reached a feverish pitch. There were continual sirens in the streets and urgent radio broadcasts as the military took control of the country. Those sounds I could not have known would echo for me seventeen years later, in another land.

One day during this time my mother went into hysterics, crying and screaming, "Están muertos, están muertos." They are dead. They are dead. She put my little brother, José Hugo, and me in her bedroom. Mother explained to us that Dad and our sister had probably been killed. It seems Dad had learned that a giant labor strike was planned that would guarantee a showdown between the Peronistas and their opponents. He had gotten in his car and gone to pick up my sister at school and bring her home. It should have taken a half-hour. But five hours later my father and sister still hadn't returned.

It was only later that my distraught mother learned what

had happened. On the way back home, my had sister suffered a terrible nose-bleed. Dad took her to the hospital, but so many people had been injured in the labor confrontation that Dad and Ana María had had to wait for hours to get her in to see a doctor. The telephone and electricity were out in the area and Dad had had no way to contact Mom.

When the two finally came home, late that night, it was as if our future had been sealed.

In the following weeks, I remember my parents whispering every night in long, emotional conversations. Something was happening. One evening, they called us in and said we were going for a visit to Chile to meet our Grandma and Grandpa and all our other cousins. Chile, they said, was a beautiful country on the other side of the mountains. They reminded me that I had been there as a baby when Mom had taken me there on a trip when I was a year old.

"You'll love it," Dad said. "People are very friendly. They are not cold like Argentineans. You guys are going to be so happy." My sister asked if the people in Chile spoke the same language and dressed the same. Dad painted a picture that was the equivalent of Disneyland today — a child's paradise.

But it turned out that not all of us in the family were going to leave Argentina.

Amid the political upheaval that had opened a chasm in the country, there came an outbreak of polio. One day in July, I was playing with little José Hugo. We lined up chairs to play bus. He fell and hit his head hard. That night, Mom kept an eye on him. She always had premonitory dreams. Like most Latin women, she believed powerfully in the spirit world. In the middle of the night I suddenly heard her in hysterics. Doors slammed, then the garage door opened and the car motored off.

Mom checked on my brother and noticed his eyes were white. She gathered him up and took off on foot toward a neighborhood clinic. Dad dressed and drove off after her. He picked her up and, together, they drove to the clinic. The doctor decided that the only option was surgery. It was unknown whether my brother was having a polio attack or was simply suffering some after-effect of his fall. The clinic was severely undermanned. Some nurses were on strike; what staff remained were overwhelmed by the influx of injured demonstrators. A skeleton team prepared my brother for surgery. He was about to be taken to the operating room when the facility suffered a complete power outage that lasted through the night.

They could not help him. And so my little brother died.

From that day on, as young as I was, I knew that political unrest claims as its martyrs not merely those who posture and would hold themselves up as heroes, but — in much larger numbers — society's most helpless.

In March 1957, the remaining four of us moved to Chile. We were turning a new page. Mom got pregnant not long after my brother's death. As we crossed the Andes, she was carrying a new child inside. My parents continued referring to our move as a "vacation," and, in fact, we left almost all our possessions behind. I wanted to take my guitar, but Dad told me to leave it since "we would be coming back in a month." But we would never go back to live in Argentina. Not until after we arrived in Santiago did Mom learn that father had sold the factory in Mendoza and signed a contract to manage a battery factory in Santiago.

Santiago stretched out like an enormous city to a little girl who had grown up in a rural farming town. Chile was and is a land of contrasts. Ninety percent of the adult population is literate, an incomparable feat among South American nations. However, the gulf between the haves and have-nots is wide, indeed. It is a classic situation. With wealth and opportunity concentrated in the cities, the poor rural population migrates to urban areas, ringing them with impoverished shantytowns that the Chileans call "callampas," mushrooms.

These belts of destitution were foreign to us. The first time we visited the shop father now managed, it proved an incredible shock. Mendoza was small, clean, pure. Santiago was large, smoggy and crowded — a sensory overload for a little girl from the Argentinean countryside. I believe it was even frightening for Mom, who had never lived in a big city.

I also was impressed that the majority of people were comparatively dark-skinned; I thought to myself that I fit in, already. I was quickly to learn otherwise.

It is surprising how much neighboring Spanish-speaking countries can exist as culturally distinct societies. My linguistically distinct Chilean relatives had quick fun with us, demanding that Ana María and I speak, and then laughing uproariously at our Argentinean accents. It took very few incidents of ridicule before my sister and I were afraid to speak to anyone other than our parents. We were absolutely appalled by the cruel fact that our manner of communicating set us up for being instantly disliked and dismissed by the people of this new country.

But we had precious little time to accustom ourselves to this startling humiliation. As soon as we had rented a house in Santiago, mother enrolled us in a private Catholic school where Ana María went into the third grade, and I was placed in first grade despite the fact I hadn't gone to school in Argentina. Not only did I not know how to read or write, my accent and attire made my assimilation even more difficult. Mom had allowed my hair to grow long. She braided and coiled it so that it resembled two telephone receivers covering my ears. She topped off this coiffure with big white bows. Since I was very skinny and short as well as odd-looking, I was an easy target for the cruel jokes of the Chilean first graders.

That same year, border conflicts flared between Chile and Argentina. I was too young to understand then, but the traditional reason for border skirmishes between two Latin American nations is political unrest in either of the nations, or both. In response to domestic problems such as runaway inflation or social agitation, government leaders seek to divert public attention by fomenting diplomatic and military skirmishes centered on old, vague boundary disputes.

Children are far from immune to these passions. Thus, my

new Chilean classmates were suddenly infected with the "let's fight Argentina" fever. I became an even less sympathetic newcomer in their midst. I was a bewildered 7-year-old caught in the middle of these natural and artificial conflicts. Ana María and I became those "dirty Argentineans."

Because of this anti-Argentinean sentiment, we were forbidden to sit and gaze out the windows at our house. I remember the whole place was kept very dark. We were counseled not to talk to strangers. Our parents picked us up from school and drove us immediately home.

It seems absurd now; but back then, given the upheaval we had endured in our lives, we merely took it in stride. That May, Mom gave birth to a son named after his deceased brother: José Hugo. We daughters remained securely sheltered from Santiago's teeming, downtrodden masses. We were enrolled in an exclusive, upper-class, private girls' school, Universitario El Salvador. The school prepared young women for college. The nuns from Ireland were stern. Our uniforms with hats and ties were very European. The curriculum was all culture, sophistication and discipline imported from Europe to nurture our privileged caste.

I should have felt fortunate, yet the school environment oppressed me. I arrived as an outcast, set adrift in this strange new world, with my dopey-rolled hair, my funny Argentinean Spanish and my inability to even scrawl numerals or letters. Fortunately, I attracted a savior of sorts. A petite nun, Sister Consuelo, attached herself to me as my protector. She proved to be a godsend since the older children saw me and Ana María as easy targets for physical attacks. My sister learned to defend herself very quickly, but I was scared of everything, being petite, younger and skinny. I was at a distinct disadvantage.

My sister had another advantage over me: she was pale-complexioned like most of the other students in the school. The majority of students were of European ancestry. I inherited different genes, clearly the Indian blood of Mom's mother, and now in the first grade I was made to be quite conscious of my olive hue. To be dark, I found out, was to be regarded as inferior.

It strikes me now as remarkable how children immediately associate themselves with peers suffering a shared social stigma. My best friends became the children of Arab ancestry who, like me, were dusky-skinned. They had surnames such as Manzur or Awad; yet the others referred to them as "Indians." And so I was misled to believe they actually were Indians from Chile. I, too, however, was called "Indian" many times. It was meant as an insult. To be called Indian was to be called stupid.

We "Indians" soon formed our own group. It included a few Jewish girls whose families had converted to Catholicism. They were subject to ridicule, too. If you didn't want to buy a piece of candy for someone, you were called "Jewish." I quickly learned the myths that governed my little world: stupid people were "Indians" and cheap people were "Jewish."

Fortunately for me, however, I did adapt to the new Chilean culture very rapidly. In no time I had lost my Argentinean accent and was conversing like a Chilean. Despite my appearance, I was able to read and write by summer vacation that begins at Christmastime in Chile. This progress I owed to Sister Consuelo. During recess, while the other children went outside to play, she would tutor me in the numbers and letters.

I very quickly fell in love with the more outgoing Chilean culture and became one hundred percent Chilena. Mom used to say I was the one who became a Chilena first. I became fully part of the school too. Universitario El Salvador was a very academically demanding institution. It produced well-rounded students. I participated in sports — I was a sprinter and even played basketball. I dabbled in guitar and wrote poetry and loved the arts. I was involved with school theater. The school nurtured a highly motivated atmosphere; we'd take field trips to the opera, the symphony or art museums. There was nothing lacking in our exposure to upper-class culture, and to a first-rate academic education.

When I was ten years old, my father left Mom for a younger

woman for the first of many times. Divorce was unheard of in Catholic Chile; so was legal separation. Even so, I'm not sure that Mom would have divorced him even if it were permitted. As it happened, Dad returned to Mom a couple of years later when he became interested in politics and recognized the importance of a solid, family-man image.

In his political life, Dad's earliest predisposition was to help the downtrodden masses of his country. Although his basic nature changed dramatically over the next twenty years, my social consciousness was indelibly formed during this period and by events in the summer of my 14th year.

That summer we were at my paternal grandfather's ranch, in Rancagua, when an incident occurred that forever impressed me. It punctured like a knife the sheltered world view that had been nurtured in the confines of my exclusive private school.

These large *fundos* or ranches were spotted with small adobe homes that had corrugated roofs and often no doors. Here the workers and their families lived. As we learned to ride horses, Ana María and I would trot down to the homes and visit the people who would welcome my sister and me effusively because we were the grandchildren of the patron. They were fascinated with us because we were from the city, a place many of them had never visited. I soon realized that these workers were up laboring before sunrise and didn't quit until the sun went down. They worked without receiving benefits other than their temporary "homes," a little bit of money, and a little area where they could plant crops to feed themselves. They received no significant salary or any other benefit. They were share-croppers.

My sudden awakening to the inequities of the economic system was the beginning of my political conscience. It radicalized my thinking to compare my upper-class, cloistered Catholic school existence with the misery of the farming class. *Los inquilinos*, "the renters," were families whose children had no hope of attending school because they were put to work in the fields early in life.

Each Friday, the workers lined up for their pay. They'd receive a hard loaf of bread (*galleta*) and a few "pesos" in wages. One day, an *inquilino* inquired about a raise. The supervisor took him out of the line and beat him mercilessly. The poor peasant was then fired, and told to leave the ranch immediately. Despite my innocence, I knew how devastating this dismissal was for him and his family. With no benefits, he had no safety net. He was put onto a *carretela*, a horse-led cart, and ordered to vacate his hovel that night. He loaded his family and belongings and left. He was jobless, penniless and homeless, with no one to speak for him.

Dad had returned to Mom when I was twelve. His politics and public image was rooted in the conservatism of a landowner and a dynamic entrepreneur who had carved out a lucrative niche in the marketplace with his battery factory. Yet Dad's hungry and far-reaching spirit made him inclined to extend a hand to the working class. In truth, I don't think he appreciated the way his father dealt with *los inquilinos* on his ranch.

Dad was not a human being to turn a blind eye to reality. His days as a rambunctious *huaso* wedded to the terrain were too deeply embedded in him to ignore the plight of simple people contending with the land, in an eternally discouraging battle to scratch out a subsistence. He first got involved in the progressive Christian Democrat party and rose high in its ranks. He worked close to Eduardo Frey during that presidential candidate's successful campaign. Dad became firmly entrenched in the political machine. Naturally, friction resulted between him and his conservative father. But for me, Dad's involvement with the Christian Democrats was absolutely exhilarating. While Ana María had absolutely no interest in these affairs, I couldn't get enough. There I was, in the very middle of a great movement to right our country's wrongs. The consuming guilt of my privileged adolescence seemed to melt away, to be replaced by the earnestness of action every time I accompanied Dad to campaign headquarters to stuff envelopes, or when I carried signs at political rallies.

In 1964 Eduardo Frey was elected president of Chile. He began limited land reform. His theoretical tack was to break up some of the large *fundos* and apportion land to *los inquilinos*. But Chile didn't begin to see tangible effects of the agrarian reform until almost a decade later when Dr. Salvador Allende was elected president.

It was a whole new phase of Chilean government. The previous administration had been that of Jorge Alessandri who headed the staunchly right-wing Conservative party. Frey laid the groundwork for liberal reform that built like a slow but irresistible tide throughout the 1960s, not ending until the cataclysmic events of 1973.

What I had seen with my own eyes that summer when I was fourteen made me favor the move to empower the peasants mired in crushing economic servitude. I had no political or ideological basis on which to justify my feelings; I just knew deep inside myself that something had to be done. By the end of high school, I was firmly committed to the government's principle of uplifting the lower classes. The status quo simply could not continue. I fully supported the liberalization of farm ownership as well as the other changes that were taking place in the late 1960s.

In 1965, a year after Frey's victory, Santiago held municipal elections. Dad ran for a city council seat in the heart of the capital's slums. It was a dirty campaign. Dad proved himself a charismatic speaker. He aimed his speeches at the impoverished electorate. Unfortunately, his liberal bent earned him disdain within his own class. He did not prevail.

Despite the losing campaign I was quickly smitten by the heady drug of politics, which overwhelmed even the gross incongruities of the run for office. Dad, for example, presented himself as a family man. My sister and brother, Mom and I would be positioned at the front of the stage, dressed up cutely and smiling, while Dad's musical words resounded over the throng. However, we knew that he had several mistresses and would not come home for days at a time because he had a "casa chica," another women with children. Still, I knew he cared greatly about the plight of the working class. He concentrated his campaign, however, on the more practical issues of fighting inflation and improving education.

The issue of crime was never an emotional lightning rod for politicians to exploit in Chile in those years. How could one focus on crime when people were dying of hunger? Instead, Dad argued economics. How could Chile hope for wide-sweeping prosperity when inflation was out of control and prices kept going up and up every day? First we must thwart and reverse inflation, then all the other long-needed social transformations would take place, he said. Stopping inflation and extending education to the masses was the way to win the war on poverty, Dad said.

I dreamed of being able to deliver stirring speeches like him. He always spoke from outlines. His large voice quickly commanded an audience and swept it with intoxicating phrases that elicited excited applause. When he traveled through the shantytowns that composed his would-be constituency, I sometimes accompanied him, often scared to death. It was common knowledge in my school that venturing into *las callampas* would invite certain death at the hands of the disadvantaged.

Indeed, I did encounter the deepest poverty there. I hadn't even heard that such destitution existed in my own city. There were naked children in one-room cardboard homes where ten people lived. Sometimes I saw homes with fifteen people to a room, and no one was certain who exactly the children's fathers were. It seemed as if every naked child had a runny nose and every woman was pregnant. There was no way out for any of them because there were no jobs and no social programs. Proper plumbing and sanitation were more remote than if they existed only on Mars. Fleas and lice abounded. The streets were unpaved, and because it was winter the soil had turned to mud. Walking down these roads was repulsive. The overriding smell was of open sewers.

Coming face-to-face with the city's burgeoning poor proved to be a graphic rebuke to the Catholic tenet we had been taught that contraception was evil. Just as my exposure to the workers' conditions at my grandfather's ranch had forever shattered my blissful world and generated my sudden consciousness about the need for agrarian reform, the dogma of the Catholic Church that had been inculcated at school now seemed like such a cruel lie.

Despite Dad's incessant stumping, the shantytowns did not get out the vote and he lost his election. The poor, who would benefit the greatest by liberal change, never voted in large numbers. (Today, voting is not only a right, but a requirement in Chile, as it is in Argentina.)

Dad's political orientation slowly began to shift to the right as his business fortunes grew in the ensuing years. Chile's inflation rate stabilized and the economy seemed robust, but the shantytowns that beckoned increasing numbers of the rural and uneducated poor were ticking bombs. The unemployment rate was climbing, and Santiago faced an urban nightmare of festering ghettos and no direction on how to better their lives. Chile lacked any welfare or unemployment benefits — what conservatives today term "entitlements" — for that class living below the poverty line one step from starvation. The only program the government initiated was a minimum-wage, temporary labor program for the poor on public works such as roads. Yet, the program was not sufficient. The result was an indirect employment "solution": a hidden, or underground, labor force in which the impoverished toiled in temporary menial jobs as maids, garbage collectors and the like. The only solace for the poor were the crucifixes tacked onto their cardboard walls.

After losing his first election, my father moved to a more conservative political position. At the same time, I was moving in the opposite direction to my own position.

I graduated from high school in 1968. I knew I had to attend college away from my family. My awakening political consciousness and rejection of the Catholic Church had reached the stage where I was now in full and open conflict with my father. I grew increasingly antagonistic toward him, to the point where I knew I had to leave home to find out who I was.

Nineteen sixty-eight was a year of transition across the Western Hemisphere. The children of the baby boom were everywhere questioning the ideals of their societies. The resulting tension was enormous, but to the younger generation it was the greatest challenge, and it made for the most exhilarating period of my life.

Just as U.S. teenagers shouted across the dinner tables at their parents about civil rights or the Vietnam War or drugs or long hair or rock music, Chilean youth rebelled against their parents. However, Chile was still a much more conservative country than the United States. Drugs were not part of Chilean youth culture. Possession of marijuana was a grave offense and harshly prosecuted. Dating for me in Santiago had always meant being chaperoned by my brother. But the Beatles and Rolling Stones were popular, as were long hair and vocal opposition to the U.S. military involvement in Indochina. Dad would end an angry dinnertime exchange by calling me, "Socialist!" or, "hippie!"

The anger of Chile's younger generation was almost entirely political in nature. We believed we had to make political changes to effect social changes. Let's give the poor what they've been denied! Let's fight for social justice! We came to believe we could accomplish such changes. Our movement would soon come to manifest itself in the presidential campaign of Dr. Salvador Allende. One might say the high-water mark of the entire torrent of international youth politics of the late sixties and early seventies was to crest in our South American nation in a few indescribable months in 1972.

This, however, was a few years off, and by U.S. standards, I was hardly, at age 18, the perfect budding rebel. The atmosphere of my private Catholic school had been so protective I had never heard about drugs, much less contemplated premarital sex. The place for my plunge into the wide world of ideas and adulthood was to be at the university in the coastal city of La Serena. This choice, too, was a means of rebellion.

My father said he would refuse to permit me to enroll in a college outside Santiago. I countered his move by refusing to apply to any college in Santiago. In those years, there were few options about where to go to college in Chile. Only a select group were eligible for consideration. One needed to be an excellent student, or from a reasonably wealthy background, or at least be well-connected. If you were connected, you could get an under-the-table letter that would get your name on the acceptance list.

I was accepted to the university at La Serena. I applied to go to school there because I had heard La Serena was a beautiful colonial city by the sea, and I loved the sea. Today, La Serena is one of the most popular resorts in Chile; but in those days it was so small it lacked even a large bank. La Serena's size appealed to me. As much as I wanted to be on my own, I did not want to be alone in a large city. I was not only a sheltered adolescent but a shy one, too.

When I received my letter of acceptance to La Serena, my father didn't speak to me for several days. When he finally came around, he said, "We're going to drive there." He wanted to show me how far it was from Santiago. We drove the entire day. When he, Mom and I arrived, he said, "You're on your own. We're just going to wait for you here." I trembled as I went to register for classes, looking around, bewildered about which way to go.

My father and mother had placed me into a *pension "para señoritas"* — an exclusive boarding house for young women. Rules were strict. Residents could not go out at night, and our meals, visitors and curfews were tightly monitored. My father said the only way he'd allow me to be on my own was to live at this *pension*. I accepted.

An 18-year-old away from home for the first time with questions about the correctness of her upbringing, is a prime candidate for activism. Indeed, a whole new world would quickly open up for me in La Serena.

It was to be a heady year. I became involved with students

who spoke out forcefully and knowledgeably against the United States' involvement in Vietnam. We held organizational meetings to plan protests against various decisions of the Chilean government related to the Vietnam war. In that year, I was first exposed to tear gas, and I became adept at wrapping a wet bandanna around my neck so I could quickly raise it over my face and eyes. On more than one occasion that year I would come close to being beaten by the police. One of the most remarkable experiences of the year was Allende's visit to the campus when he was campaigning for the presidency. Allende was one of the most charismatic politicians I have ever seen. He had a way of relating to young people that drew us to him. He appeared in a black turtleneck with a sports jacket and big black-framed glasses.

He spoke first in the auditorium, then he moved outside. He loved to speak out in the open, where his projecting voice needed no microphone. One could hear a pin drop in the rapt and dumbstruck throng. He signed books for the students who lined up afterward. He was a true populist, shunning bodyguards. I shook hands with Allende and couldn't sleep that night.

He spoke not only for social reform but also against the Vietnam War. He told us that he didn't want us to be like the North Americans who get involved in somebody else's business and try to control the world with their ideology. He did not agree with the policies of the U.S. government and the multinational companies, including ITT, Anaconda, the great American copper mining concern. These multinational interests were the targets of many of his speeches, and, as would unfold, he was to become the target of those same interests.

From Camelot to the Inquisition

IT WAS THE PUREST of times. It was 1969 and I was 18 years old. I lived in an all-girl "pension" with strict curfews. I studied hard and took my college courses extremely seriously (Mother had instilled in me her belief that the only thing she could really leave her children was an education). And, I joined a movement to change the world.

My embarkation toward adulthood grew beyond a standard education, beyond the intellectual pursuit of a degree. It became an enlightenment, an introduction into the rest of my country outside Santiago. My teachers were my fellow students, for whom protest seemed a duty.

At first my peers treated me as an outsider when I arrived as a college freshman. Looking back, I can understand why. Unlike them, I had come from Santiago. I was from an elite private Catholic school. I was a young woman who had decided to leave home to study in a distant city. Moreover, I had picked a profession to pursue — a college professor, a specialist in Latin American history — that was highly unusual for a woman in Chile in that time. Thus, the other students I met automatically put me on trial. They weren't sure who I was or what I stood for — this naive child of privilege, this fresh fish so obviously out of her natural waters.

Their distrust, however, changed as soon as I started to participate in political demonstrations and strikes.

My activist inclination that had been growing throughout adolescence led me to question the status quo, and ultimately drove me from my familiar nest, and now defined me in my newly chosen environment. Politics proved my route to fitting in. The people I met at La Serena had such an impact on my life.

44

Their faces float back to me still in my mind. . . .

There was Guillermo, an elementary school teacher who had returned to college to earn a higher teaching degree. I met Guillermo because we had the same major. Guillermo turned out to be one of my political mentors. He was about 30, large, dark, curly-haired — almost like a mulato. Guillermo always stood apart. He was an activist in the teacher's union; he invited me to attend meetings with him. Those "meetings" were noisy, rowdy political debates, filled with shouting and cigarette smoke. I learned as much in those meetings as I did in any classroom.

Also, even now I can still see María Cristina, who came from a little town, Vicuña, where Gabriela Mistral, the Nobel prize-winning poet, was born. Like Guillermo, María Cristina was a member of the Socialist party. After we became friends, she would take me to her home in Vicuña, which sits in the Valle del Elqui, in the north of Chile. María Cristina's parents were elementary school teachers. Although her parents were educators and their daughter was attending college, they lived differently from what I expected. I was shocked when I arrived for my first weekend at her house. The family house had dirt floors, even in the bedroom.

I have never forgotten the big cavity she had in a front tooth. I would never have dared to have had an unfilled cavity — or imagined anyone going through life like that. The world I was now seeing was the other Chile — the larger Chile, and I was moved by the contrast of these different worlds. While Chile had "socialized medicine," adequate care was not available for everyone. It was available for those who could afford it or wait, often years, for it.

My baptism into the world of political ideas had come during my first few days in college. In the midst of a classroom discussion in the Latin American history course, some students loudly denounced the Catholic Church. They charged it had oppressed women, forced them not to take contraceptives, prevented divorce from being legal in Chile, held women back and kept them down. I was dumbstruck. These criticisms of the Catholic Church would have been sacrilegious at my high school or in my parent's social circle.

I also discovered that what I had learned about the history of Chile was incomplete. I had learned traditional Chilean history: we had gained independence from Spain; fought against Peru and won; and established ourselves as a Latin power. Based on my traditional learning, I spoke proudly about Chile's fights with Bolivia and Peru and our territorial gains, and how we had helped the native Indians.

"We have given the Araucanos an incredible opportunity," I chirped, in regard to one of our Indian tribes. "We have given them homes in the south, where they had always lived in tents. We're allowing them to go to college." I was so proud of my government for helping these poor indigenous people.

I was immediately chided and scoffed at by my classmates.

"We're killing their culture!" they said.

"We're destroying what they always had. We don't teach their language. We are undermining their families."

Such opinions seemed nearly unanimous in the room. They were held as staunchly as foregone conclusions.

I also learned in those classes that the Spaniards were not necessarily the saviors who had brought civilization and high culture to Chile. It was here I heard Christopher Columbus painted as an invader and destroyer, a tyrannical and heartless imperialist, rather than a hero.

The cafeteria became the venue where we shared ideas before and after classes. Our little group would sit at a table sipping coffee and arguing. At first, the other group members were suspicious of me. They refrained from speaking of politics while I was around. Little by little, though, I became one of them. They came to trust me, sensing the admiration I felt toward them. Indeed, I thought they were leading incredible lives.

Throughout Latin America, college students have traditionally been the force to carry the torch of political activism and change in their countries. I believed I had discovered my people.

I had found my place. Ironically, at the very moment I was spreading my wings to inherit the wind of progressivism, my classmates chose me as their nominee for the competition to select the equivalent of the university's homecoming queen. *La Fiesta de los Mechones* ("*mechones*" referring to rookies) is an event geared to first-year students. It is an initiation party that included upper-class students. The competitions held between various majors became a point of pride for each class to win. The two weeks of athletic competitions and celebrations were meant to be all in fun, but were taken seriously by all.

At 18, I did little to beautify my appearance. I barely wore makeup. Yet Guillermo, my leftist friend, proposed me as the class nominee for homecoming queen. His nomination was greeted with boisterous delight by all the men in the class. "Yeah, yeah! Emma can do it!"

I called and told Mom how embarrassed I was by their behavior. She tried to put it in perspective and even added a positive spin: "Hey, maybe this is the way for you to start to fit in."

I went back the next day and told Guillermo I would accept the nomination. In retrospect, I am certain that he was not trying to put me down by nominating me. He wanted me to use my looks so the class could win and the students would get free tickets to sport competitions and social functions.

I still have the photographs of being dressed up and appearing in public, making a fool of myself. Photos of the contestants were displayed around the small town and appeared in the local newspaper. It was a beauty contest, though, thankfully, without swimsuits, but just as disgusting.

What or who really got me going on politics during those years was Guillermo. He worked as a teacher in the morning and went to university classes in the afternoon. One day, he came into the cafeteria and said, "We're going to go on strike. The only way we can press the university to meet our needs is to go on strike en masse," he said of his fellow teachers. "If we stop the teaching, then the administrators will have to realize how instrumental we are." He went down the list of teachers' complaints, including insufficient salaries and benefits.

It was at that moment that our discussion group began to talk in earnest about what was right and wrong with our country. I didn't say anything at first. But when the discussion shifted to agrarian reform, I spoke with conviction about the need for it. I recounted my story of the *inquilino* who had asked for a raise and then been brutally beaten and evicted. The others were surprised. This product of a Catholic school, of upper-middle class Santiago, had true feelings based on experience.

I spoke out with equal zeal on women's issues. I told them that even though I had been baptized and raised a Catholic and that two of my aunts were nuns and my grandfather's uncle had been an Archbishop in Italy, I had serious doubts about the Church's positions on many women's issues, especially abortion.

I told them about one of my best friends in high school who had an illegal abortion the year before. It was the first time I had been able to mention this dark episode to anyone.

My friend had been dating a boy from Argentina. He would come to Chile every summer. Sex was a taboo subject at our Catholic school, and so the rest of us had no clue that the two were so involved.

"You know, I'm pregnant," she told me one day.

"I cannot tell my parents," she said. "I cannot tell anybody at school. I have to have an abortion."

Abortion. That was the first time in my life I had even considered the issue. The word was practically foreign to me.

"Well," I finally said to her, "it's only right. If you don't want to have it, you shouldn't have it. We'll go the doctor, then we'll go to the hospital."

My friend quickly corrected me. "It's against the law," she said.

Then another of our friends intervened. She told us that she had heard through her family's maid about how a woman could go to a shantytown and pay to have an abortion. A few days later, the three of us set off after school, in our uniforms, for the address we had gotten from the maid. The location was in a shantytown outside Santiago.

We were frightened. But we gamely climbed into a taxi and the driver eventually located the address. An old woman answered our knock. She made us wait outside while our friend was taken to a back room. After no more than 20 minutes, our friend rejoined us. We hailed a cab to take us home.

"It was very simple," she explained to us on the ride home. "She injected something in me, parsley, like a little tampon, and said it would take care of it." The old woman had cautioned her that the parsley would cause her to bleed and she should return the next day.

By the next day, my dear friend was screaming in pain at school.

"I've started my period," she told me.

After school, we returned to the old woman's address. Standing outside, my other friend and I heard the most incredible screams coming from within. They were brutal, and we felt helpless. We were barred from the room. When our pregnant friend finally came out, her face was that of a different woman than had first entered the room. She told us that the old lady had used homemade tools, like spoons, to stop the bleeding and clean her out.

The following day, she didn't show up at school. When I came home, Mom said that my friend's mother had telephoned. My friend was in the hospital, unconscious. She was suffering from a terrible infection.

When her parents found out about the abortion, we were automatically viewed as accomplices, perhaps even the instigators of their daughter's catastrophe. After this ugly episode, I promised myself to do everything to preserve a woman's right to a safe abortion.

My college friends were moved by my story. I began accompanying them to meetings at the student center. The topics of these meetings never concerned how we could advance our careers as future professionals. Instead, everything was geared toward, "what can we do to better our country?" Frequently, the talk turned militant.

Things began heating up when student elections were held. Far from being isolated from real world politics, student candidates for college offices had to announce their party affiliations — Socialist, Christian Democrat, Radical, National, and so on. In those years at the university, it was an embarrassment to be part of the Conservative party, *El Partido Nacional*. It would have meant being branded a pig. During that time, I had to examine my own political persuasion. I was vacillating between the Christian Democrats and the Socialists. I didn't like the Communist party because, according to my views, it was extremist and stifled personal growth. I was liberal, but not radical. Yet, it turned out such distinctions would prove insignificant in a polarized nation.

The same student interest that permeated the U.S. campuses in 1969 and 1970 was in full bloom in Chile. In that year we began to organize our political campaign for Dr. Salvador Allende.

Allende was no newcomer to national politics. Although he had lost elections for the presidency before, he was a passionate candidate and a great speaker, and provided the right song for our ears. A member of the Socialist party, Allende formed a coalition of parties, *La Unidad Popular*, among the Communist and Radical parties. This arrangement created a schism in the larger, more centrist, Christian Democrat party. The resulting splinter factions needed to sign up members. I joined one of these Christian Democrat party factions, the MAPU — *el partido de Movimiento de Acción Popular Unida*. MAPU was the more left-leaning faction of the Christian Democrats, my father's party.

Huge political rallies became a regular occurrence. The campus became utterly politicized. If I went to a social function and someone asked me to dance, he would ask what party I belonged to before he would ask my name. We students were breathing politics.

At first, my parents knew nothing of my political activity. Finally, during a stay at home, I discussed some of my beliefs with my father. He was disgusted to learn that I had become a member of MAPU and that I would support Allende. To my father, Allende was a dangerous man even if no one expected him to win.

But I knew Allende would win. I was so caught up in his campaign, I never wavered in this faith. Allende who would bring social justice to the downtrodden of my country! Allende would oppose *Yanqui* imperialism in Chile and the world! Allende who was the powerful, clear voice of change for Chile!

In 1970, when Allende was elected president, running on a program to make Chile socialist, he would become the first democratically elected Socialist to head up a state in the Western Hemisphere. All of a sudden, the dream we had would become reality. We believed that we would first change Chile, then the world. Our Allende was going to be the historical figure that introduced peaceful socialism to not only Chile but also to the rest of the Third World. We all felt the inevitability of that outcome.

For him, we would have done anything. We worked for his campaign for nothing more than the dream of seeing him elected. My political awakening five years before on my paternal grandfather's ranch had become a passion during my father's campaign, and that passion was now consumed in Allende's attempt to change the world. Politics would never again smell as sweet.

We progressive students disseminated pamphlets for our candidate at rallies. We posted campaign signs everywhere, mixing flour and water for paste, plastering Allende's face wherever we could, even where it was illegal to post bills on walls. We'd paste up Allende's signs and remove whatever opponents' likenesses happened to be in our path. How ironic that the student supporters of my opponent in my campaign twenty-five years later would use the same tactic and would get paid to do it.

Election Day, September 4, 1970, was a surprise. The race was too close to call. No candidate enjoyed a majority, but

Allende emerged with the most votes. My discussion group was at the library when we heard the news. We immediately headed off to celebrate.

We went to a favorite hangout to eat *completos*, the Chilean hot dogs laden with avocado, then held a party. Our elation bordered on euphoria, but it was clouded at the edges by the knowledge that Chile's Congress would have to confirm Allende as president.

In the following weeks, the right wing injected an element of paranoia into the national debate. Radio ads and newspaper columns supported by the CIA were filled with this invective: Did we want a Communist to lead Chile? Would the rich be fleeced in the name of giving to the poor? Some wealthy Chileans did not wait around to find out. They sold their homes and left the country, sending money overseas into Swiss bank accounts.

The lawmakers approved Allende. The age of idealism had begun. It was a time not of innocence but of purity, the likes of which my generation would never see again.

I began a journey not unlike that of my grandfather Sylvestre Pulvirenti when he set off to the New World. He sought to carve out an empire of wealth and comfort while I sought social justice in the land where my roots were planted. Both of us had sought paradise. Such are the conceits of youth. But are they not more noble than the calloused conventions of what we deem maturity?

In the next few years of my life, a whole nation would find out.

There, in La Serena, we students felt as if the dream had become real. We were a part of a new page of history being written. The mood was hardly as benign back home in Santiago. My mother was practically in mourning. When I visited, she'd tell me horror stories about Socialism and Communism. "Oh, you know, in Cuba little kids have to go and get in line for an ice cream so they can have milk in their diet."

I'd listen to my parents and their friends bemoan Chile's imminent demise. Friends of mine from high school declared how awful the agrarian reform was. They spoke with trepidation about how Allende was going to make Chile into a Russian colony. We would all have to quit school and work for the government — for no pay — they said. You just wait and see. It was only a matter of time before this scoundrel Allende seized the factories and turned them over to the workers. All our futures were going to be determined by the government. Their fears felt real, palpable even.

I traversed two separate worlds. There was my family's panic-stricken circle in Santiago; and my student circle in La Serena — where we were feasting on beautiful thoughts of a shining new era to come.

Allende's stance on nationalizing Chile's copper industry captivated me. Copper was Chile's main natural resource. There were American companies, Anaconda and ITT, exploiting this resource. Yet these companies were removing this natural resource from our country as fast as they could, not caring that the miners who toiled to extricate it could barely survive on their wages and labored under extremely perilous conditions. We studentsl believed that these North American imperialists had come to Chile to strip us of our riches while not even attempting to learn our language or assimilate into our culture (no green cards either!).

Allende's move for agrarian reform also appealed to me. I didn't see it as arbitrarily confiscating land from ranchers and handing it over to tenant farmers, because I was all too familiar with the pressing need of the *inquilinos* for worker protection and better wages. I knew something had to be done. I felt the same when it came to big industry. Many companies were paying miserable salaries to laborers. Allende was going to correct this, granting more rights to the working class. Society as a whole would benefit.

I held another hope for reform: since women were going to

be instrumental in the new work force, maybe their rights would be expanded. Maybe we would gain at least the right to choose a better job. Maybe in Allende's Chile, there would be a push for equality of the sexes. There might even be room to change the divorce and abortion laws.

To us students who had devoted ourselves to the cause of justice, the world seemed awash in new hope. Cuban president Fidel Castro came to Santiago's National Stadium to speak. My classmates and I went to hear him. I found Castro to be very bright and charismatic even though I didn't accept his communist ideas.

Castro, standing on stage with Allende, said he wanted to congratulate Chile for peacefully selecting socialism. Castro declared that Allende's democratic election marked an incredible moment in history. The rest of his speech, though, was lost on me. He kept talking about how the people must sacrifice as individuals for the betterment of the country. I noted that Castro had been sacrificing his own people for ten years with little to show for it. All Cuba had was hemispheric political isolation and hardship for the people. I disliked how he spoke so strongly against those who had gained economic power. It seemed, even then, all too simplistic. I didn't believe that you could just take from the rich and give to the poor and expect to call it justice. As full of youthful idealism as I was, I could still see many flaws in his plans.

But there is nothing like the pristine optimism at the beginning of a new governmental administration. A supporter only thinks of all that can go right.

For Allende, however, all the right things were to go wrong.

Allende had come to power with a political coalition. Almost immediately, the coalition began to unravel. One of Allende's first acts was to nationalize the copper industry. The mines were to be controlled by the Chilean government. The big multinational corporations proved to be no weak sisters, however. They were formidable foes. The result of Allende's move to take over the mines was a U.S. trade boycott slapped on Chile. The economy took a licking.

The coalition began to disintegrate. MIR *(el Movimiento de Izquierda Revolucionario)* — the Leftist Revolutionary Movement — declared that the existing Communist and Socialist parties that backed Allende were too conservative. Allende disagreed and the MIR began their own movement for changes.

The biggest defeat came when Allende failed to secure basic consumer goods such as flour and oil. Some believed that the producers were deliberately holding back to sow discontent among the masses and sabotage Allende's rule. Whatever the cause, the government was fast finding itself in an untenable position.

To meet the consumer crisis, the government issued a national food card. Food could only be purchased with this card. This created intense anger among the middle class. My mother refused to stand in line and ask for this card. She would buy what goods she could; but she would *not obey* this order from the government. Insecurity about the ability to get food became widespread. Business strikes were crippling the economy. Confrontations in the streets between workers and police became a regular scene.

I was somewhat removed from all this at La Serena, the small seaside town that did not suffer the discord going on in the rest of the country. However, by the end of 1972, I had transferred to the University of Chile in Santiago. I had decided that I wanted to go to a larger school, to earn my degree from a more prestigious institution. When I got to Santiago, I discovered how out-of-control things had become. The Allende spring had become a bitter winter. As the situation deteriorated, my family history — what befell us in Argentina — began to repeat itself.

In July 1973, my second brother, José Hugo, was seriously injured in a car accident while driving with some friends. The country was in such a state of turmoil by now, hospital workers were on strike. The only factory that produced intravenous fluid also was on strike. Even doctors were divided along party lines.

A Communist would not treat a Nationalist. It was chaos. The night José Hugo was taken to an emergency care unit, he received almost no attention.

For a week, my father fought in vain to locate the intravenous fluid for my brother and a physician to operate on my brother's head injury.

The political gulf had widened so extremely it even divided families. Two of my aunts were dentists and belonged to the Socialist party. My father, in desperation, telephoned one to see if she could use her connections to enable José Hugo to be transferred to a hospital that specialized in head injuries.

"Well, call one of your Christian Democrat friends," she told him.

So, like his namesake brother before him, José Hugo died amidst the screams and blindness of political fratricide. Again in my life, I saw how easily politics claims its victims from the ranks of society's most helpless. My parents blamed Allende for my brother's death — but the truth was the nation was simply polarized. Its key institutions were paralyzed. Hostility ran rampant.

It was clear what side of the wall I was caught on.

My new university, like La Serena, remained a stalwart backer of Allende. Our professors were heavily politicized, and they were liberals. "Now, we're going to read the Marxist version of the history of Chile," an emphatic instructor would tell our class. My new campus was dubbed, "the Red School." And, I believe, I was rapidly becoming more conservative as I attended student meetings and faced the hot rhetoric of the radicals. The word from them was that the military was preparing to seize control of the government; we needed to take up arms to defend ourselves.

I was a liberal within the law. I didn't believe confiscating all the land from the rich and giving it to the poor was the solution, either. I thought the government had to educate the people before granting them land, and educate the worker about his rights instead of taking over a factory and telling him he now owned it, even though he'd never managed one before. I was fast becoming a political outsider on my new campus. My dating an American didn't help, either.

Michael was eight years older than I, a typical blond-haired, All-American, white Anglo-Saxon Protestant. He'd come to Chile five years earlier as a Peace Corps volunteer, become fluent in Spanish and stayed on as an employee of the Cooperative for American Relief Everywhere (CARE). He helped distribute food and other necessities to the impoverished.

Michael believed there were better ways for Chile to develop into a strong democracy than to submit to rule by a coalition of leftists. When my friends learned of his beliefs, some of them accused me of being involved with a CIA agent.

Michael and I dated six months, but when he asked me to marry him, I was shocked. I kept the proposal secret from my family. I had the summer off from the university, from December through March, and my sister who was living in Venezuela asked me to spend the summer there. I needed a breather. I would be graduating soon.

My mother and father picked me up at the airport upon my return from Venezuela. We got in the car. I told them, "Michael asked me to marry him when I left. I have thought about it for the last three months and I'm going to marry him." Despite their own history of flouting parental wishes, neither my father nor mother supported my decision, since Michael was a foreigner.

I tried to reassure, "Hey, we're not going to go and live in the United States."

In 1973, while still at college, I worked in a small school, *la Escuela Consolidada*, in a suburb of Santiago. The controversial school was for kids who weren't easy to control, and for older kids who had flunked out of the traditional high schools. It was a technical school where students studied the trades, such as bookkeeping. However, the older students were very politically attuned. Teaching them history proved complicated, given the extreme passions of the day. Discussing the labor movement, for example, was almost impossible; interpreting events could favor either side in the national debate. Students in the classrooms, like their country, were divided between pro- and anti-government factions. And they were shrill about their views.

It became increasingly difficult to control the classroom. Sometimes students would punch each other and I'd have to separate them. Looking back, I am sure I was rather comical, a petite, twenty-two-year-old in a mini-skirt, trying to maintain order, stepping between two large teenage boys slugging it out. Sometimes I had to run to the principal for help. Occasionally, police would show up on campus.

It was no learning environment.

Political rallies in La Serena had been fun. In Santiago, I learned your life could end at one. Chaos was now everywhere. The streets of Santiago regularly swelled with protesters. Then a force of police would arrive and the tear gas would start. It could take one or two hours to simply commute to or from work by public transportation, and the commute could sometimes be dangerous. One day, during one of the frequent bus strikes, a man opened the hood of the bus I was on and tossed a grenade into the engine. The explosion caused sheer panic, with passengers fleeing for the doors. Amazingly, no one was killed.

One familiar sight in Santiago that year were the *Guanacos*. These are large police trucks with water tanks. Riot police would hose down the streets, and the force of the spray knocked people flat to the ground. If you were caught in the wrong place at the wrong time, you could get clobbered. I did several times.

I also learned that the greatest casualty of political turmoil is human dignity. The political parties in the Popular Unity became so embroiled in their own little disputes, they forgot about what was in the best interest of the people. What was most important, what they had supposedly been struggling for, became secondary.

I learned one other thing: how powerful the United States of America can be in deciding the destiny of other countries. As matters seemed to be approaching a climax, I began noticing on campus people I did not recognize, speaking English. Rumors about CIA infiltration were rampant, as they were about the CIA fomenting unrest in worker strikes. MIR members insisted the CIA was coming. Looking back, I do remember times when a "reporter" would appear to take photographs of groups of students at rallies. Who knows if they truly were journalists? The confusion and growing hysteria seemed just one more part of the continuing collapse. The only thing that seemed certain was that nothing was heading in a positive direction.

Then, almost as if scripted in a play, the upper-class women took to the streets against Allende, shouting that he was destroying the future of their children, that he was too weak to stand up to the Communist party and that Chile would become another Cuba. They circulated petitions asking for the resignation of Allende. They gathered in massive protests, clanging empty pots and pans with their diamond-adorned fingers, declaring they had no food. It was so ironic that the richest were now claiming to be the poorest.

The last group to go on strike were the truck drivers. Chile is a geographically long country that must rely on truck transportation for food distribution. Most truck-company owners were from the lower middle-class and felt they could not afford to go out on strike. Yet, these same small business owners finally did go out on strike.

It seemed that someone else was financing them. Later, it became clear that the Nixon administration was using the CIA and other groups to squeeze Chile's democratically elected government into submission. My father had the view that this outside influence was necessary. He was certain the government was to blame for this disastrous situation. "The United States has to come forward and help us," he said. "They are the only ones who can save us from this Marxist cancer."

At the end of August, several tanks rolled into Santiago. A showdown was imminent. We thought a military coup would happen at any moment. However, nothing more happened. The tanks stopped at a gas station, refueled and left.

September 11, I heard the news. Early on that Tuesday morning in spring, around 6 o'clock, the telephone rang. It was my father.

"Just like I told you," he said. "It's going to be a big revolution and the military is taking over. I have inside information."

"That's b.s.," I said.

"Don't go to school today, you will die," he said, in an imploring tone. I knew he was exaggerating. But I humored him. "Okay, I'll stay home," I said.

My mother was in Argentina. After my brother died, she was distraught with grief and had gone to stay with relatives. My father was now again separated from my mother and was living with another woman and her two children. I was staying at my mother's house with my husband. Michael already had left for work.

I got up and took a shower. It was about a quarter to eight in the morning, and I was almost ready to leave the house when I switched on the radio. It turned out to be a stroke of luck. I was turning the dial to find a station, when I encountered: "ta-ta, ta-ta . . ."

Martial music!

I turned to another station. More military tunes. I turned to a third station. An official voice, certainly not a disc jockey's, was announcing, "National order No. 3: everybody remain in their homes. The military is moving in. The ports are being taken over. The troops are in front of *La Moneda* (the president's palace), it is surrounded."

The audience was told that the military had taken over the governmental agencies and was reported to be in complete control of the country. The voice reported that soldiers were seizing the radio and television stations and newspapers. I was both stunned and gripped by fear.

Television programming was completely shut off. I remained glued to the radio, scared to death. I was alone. I didn't know what to do. Should I stay put? The phone rang again. It was my father.

"Be careful, the phones are tapped," he said. "Don't talk to any of your leftist friends. And don't open the windows. Remain in the back of the house. There's going to be a lot of shooting."

Indeed.

About 8:30 in the morning, gunfire began raging outside.

I had seen war depicted in movies, but I had never heard real gunfire. It was the most horrifying experience, to hear people screaming in the streets right outside my door.

My mother's house was in a neighborhood some distance from downtown, but all of Santiago seemed to be a war zone. I began hearing airplanes droning overhead. They came in low over the rooftops. The radio announced that soldiers had orders to shoot civilians who were outside. It was an effective strategy for scaring people away from hurrying to protect the seat of the democratic government at the palace.

That morning, Allende had managed to make it from his house to the palace. From there he was able to transmit a radio signal. His voice was still coming over several stations, exhorting, "Everybody go out in the streets and defend the democratic system. I was elected by you and I will give my life for you."

Confusion reigned.

Many of the workers who supported Allende did go into the streets that day and the shooting by the military followed. A rhythm of sorts developed. Military machine gun fire would fill the air, followed by the wails of ambulance sirens, then a long period of silence. A continual call-and-response.

My mother's home was a Spanish-style abode with a courtyard. I wanted to be physically as far as possible from the courtyard, where anyone entering could draw gunfire as an target. I cowered in the bedroom. The windows were shuttered. I dared not look out.

I sat close to the radio, keeping it at a low volume and trying to be as quiet as I could. I didn't want anyone to realize I was home. As the minutes marched on, Allende's voice disappeared from one frequency after another.

My father had told me over the phone that soldiers were searching homes. A thought sent a bloodcurdling drill through me: what if they were to find all my leftist music and books in the house? This same paralyzing sensation was being felt by students and leftists all over the capital that day. It was all part of the collective panic. When one of my university friends called to report that the military had poisoned the water supply, I believed her.

I now found myself a prisoner with no water and scarcely any food. The economy had become so bedraggled that one had to buy groceries on a daily basis. My refrigerator and cupboards held some milk, flour, oil, potatoes and eggs. I made some fried eggs, but noted I was running out of matches for the gas stove, so I left it on. What if I were trapped inside for days? I might starve.

Sometime around noon, Allende made his last broadcast. I moved my tape recorder next to the radio. I was, after all, a student of history and wanted to record these historic moments. At the same time, I was terrified that at any moment soldiers would burst through the front door, catch me listening to the speech and shoot me.

"Do not go out and be killed," Allende's voice said. "They have taken over. Traitors have betrayed me."

He sounded very shook up and distraught. All our dreams were fading into a bitter fog. I couldn't control my tears. He continued with a short speech. "Workers of my homeland, I have faith in Chile and its future. Other men will overcome this dark and bitter moment when treason seems dominant. You must never forget that, sooner rather than later, the grand avenues will be opened where free men will march on to build a better society. Long live Chile; long live the people; long live the workers! These are my last words, certain that the sacrifice will not be in vain. I am sure that there will be at least a moral sanction that will punish the felony, cowardice and treason."

I clung to the hope that Allende would accept the military's offer broadcast on other stations, of exile. I thought he could return when the atmosphere improved. I didn't believe he was going to go down with the ship. I nurtured this belief with all my strength.

After Allende's speech, General Augusto Pinochet came on the radio. I was surprised. This man had been supportive of Allende. Now, it turned out, he was speaking as the joint leader of the Army, Navy and Air Force, the military that had now taken over. Even the police were with the military. This, too, was a blow for me. In Chile, one grows up with incredible respect for the police. They live next to you, they protect your rights, they keep the peace. Now they had joined in evicting our legally elected leader.

What had happened to my world?

Pinochet announced that the military was giving Allende a chance to get out of the country. "We are in control of the country and we are going to bombard the palace," he said. It would be the final stroke in the takeover. Allende had until a certain hour to leave alive, before the bombs fell.

The deadline changed several times that day. Allende was told a helicopter was poised to lift him out. He still wouldn't leave the palace. The suspense was building to the breaking point.

Alone in the bedroom, I thought about my mother. She had lost another son in the midst of a nation's unrest. As if these two blows weren't cruel enough, she was sitting by a television in Argentina worrying and wondering if she would ever see her daughter again, knowing I had participated in leftist political activity for several years. There was no way I could even reach her to say I was okay. I tried to call. Nothing was getting through outside the country.

Early in the afternoon, a lull was broken by airplanes roaring overhead. This is it, I thought. I peeked through the curtains. The planes were zooming just above the roofs. I'm going to die, I thought. They're going to bomb all over the city. There was no way out of this.

It was a moment when my being was reduced to a heartbeat. A moment so concentrated I could hear my heart pounding. I groped for a pen and paper. Tears streamed down my cheeks as I wrote two brief poems. Afterward, I hid them under the bed:

EL ULTIMO REZO DE SETIEMBRE

Retorcida en el suelo
me obligaste a rezar
— Santificado sea tu nombre —
Afuera
las balas daban musica de fondo
a los gritos
los gritos seguian el ritmo
de las balas.
— Hágase señor tu voluntad —
Balas
y gritos.
— Como nosotros perdonamos
a nuestros deudores —
Solamenta balas.
....
....
Dejé de rezar.
....
....
Se me anudó la garganta
y sentí una lágrima
que crecía desde afuera
hacia adentro.
La absorbí lentamente
litro por litro
y en cuerpo y alma
me emborraché para siempre.
para no despertar

ni de noche
ni de dia
ni en la hora de este aborto final
cuando mi feto te dispare la última bala.

THE LAST PRAYER OF SEPTEMBER

Twisted on the floor
You compelled me to pray.
"Hallowed be thy name —"
Outside
the bullets were background music
to the cries
the cries followed the rhythm
of the bullets.
"Thy will be done —"
Bullets
and cries.
"As we forgive our debtors"
Just bullets.
....
....
I stopped praying.
....
....
My throat was clotted
and a lone tear
grew from the outside
toward my inside.
I absorbed it slowly
swallow by swallow
in body and spirit
made me drunk forever.
And never woke

not in night
not in day
not in the hour of this final abortion
when my fetus fires the last bullet at You.

* * *

11 DE SETIEMBRE DE 1973

VENCEREMOS!
escuché a las ocho
¡venceremos!
escuché otra vez
a las nueve

y a las diez
y a las once
ya a todas
las horas
del petrificado día

después

las voces

bajaron

flaquearon

se doblegaron

y el silencio

devoró el eco

eco   *eco*

eco   *eco*

eco   *eco*

*que sin darme
cuenta se convirtió
en el sonido de las balas
contra el cuerpo
de los vencidos.*

SEPTEMBER 11, 1973

WE SHALL OVERCOME!
I heard at eight
"we shall overcome!"
I heard again
at nine

and at ten
and at eleven
and all
the hours
in the petrified day

after

the voices

lowered

weakened

folded

and the silence

devoured the echo

echo   echo

echo   echo

echo   echo

without me realizing
it became
the sound
of bullets
against the body
of those who rose in opposition.

* * *

The planes, in fact, had but one mission. They were heading directly for the presidential palace.

Soon, I heard the most deafening explosions. Strangely, the concussions seemed like they were coming not from above, but from below. Huge tears were wrenched from my guts. It seemed all of Santiago was being bombarded. Amid a quick succession of tremendous impacts, I was certain that at any moment a shell would demolish my home.

Again, I became a heartbeat. Just as abruptly, dead silence

reigned.

The final blow to the Allende administration had been delivered. Yet to those who had just suffered through the bombing hunkered blindly in shuttered homes, the deafness of the aftermath invited nothing but overwhelming curiosity.

It was like the sudden calm following an earthquake. What had just happened? It seemed as if time had stopped. I could not help myself. I went outside and climbed up on a chair by a tree and peered over the courtyard wall. Billows of dark smoke were peeling into the sky from the direction of the palace downtown.

Inside, the radio offered no information. Just a continuing procession of military orders. DON'T GO OUT FOR FOOD. STAY WHERE YOU ARE. DO NOT OPEN YOUR WINDOWS. And the most intrusive one of all: PUT THE FLAG OUTSIDE YOUR HOUSE.

Hoisting the flag was meant to show that you did not oppose the new government. I had a big decision to make. Would I raise the banner in support of this military that was murdering the citizens of Chile? Or would I take the chance of not doing it, and invite a raid on my home?

Looking back, I was probably foolish not to obey the order. But who were these people to tell me whether to put the flag outside my home?! What was the flag supposed to stand for now, anyway? Here we were killing each other, and we were supposed to raise the flag?

Late that afternoon, a co-worker brought Michael home. We stared at each other. The suspicions welled up in my mind: what if my friends were right, and he had been part of all this?

"Where have you been?!" I cried.

Michael said he had been at the CARE office throughout the day. After the fighting subsided, a co-worker had attached a white scarf to his car's antenna and the two had driven through the military checkpoints, flashing their identification papers. It was risky. Many innocent people had been killed trying to get home, ignorant of what was going on because they hadn't turned on their radios. Michael had been luckier.

"This is incredible," he now said. "But it's okay." The country, Michael said, had been in such turmoil, it needed some kind of stability. This will not turn out so bad, he said. This state of emergency was only temporary. Nothing terrible was going to happen in the fallout. Michael believed that everything was now headed on its proper course. He was positive.

A news report came over the radio, announcing that the military had dropped bombs on the palace. All was now okay, it said. The capital was secured.

Around 10 o'clock that night, my mother managed to get through on the phone. She was sobbing. "Tell me you're okay. Tell me you're not going into the streets. People are being shot."

My mother, it turned out, knew more than I did about the situation in Santiago. She had been following broadcasts on Argentinean television. I wasn't prepared for the truth about Allende.

She told me, "Well, when they started bombarding the palace, he killed himself. They took his body out of the palace."

It wasn't until months later that I learned the president had sent his security men away so they wouldn't get killed. One bodyguard and his personal doctor remained with him until the last. It was his doctor who pronounced him dead.

There were no witnesses to Allende's supposed suicide, and I do not believe he would have taken his own life. His refusal to leave the palace indicates to me that he desired to carry on. Had he wanted to commit suicide, he would have done so much earlier that day. Instead, he had stood his ground.

After I saw the destruction of the palace, I saw how unlikely it was that Allende could have survived the aerial bombardment. Perhaps he died that way. Or perhaps he was killed by someone in the military storming the palace.

There has never been a photograph to surface showing Allende lying slain in the palace. What happened to his body was a long-time mystery. My mother told me that night that the body was removed and buried in a secret grave so that nobody would know where it was — not even his wife. Years later, after

Chile turned again toward democracy, Allende's remains were exhumed and reburied with all the honors due the president of a country.

My mother also told me that night that things were going to get worse in Chile before they would get better. The killing had been widespread. Bodies were floating in the Mapocho River in the capital. Corpses were being cleaned from the streets. Allende supporters were still holed up in government buildings, firing on the troops, she said.

The population was ordered by the military to remain inside for two days. I tried to make some bread from the milk and flour. We had little else to eat. On the third day, the government allowed people two hours to leave their homes and buy food. Soldiers were everywhere. At the stores, people were fighting over a rotten tomato. It was so depressing to see people who had lived near me for years contesting for a piece of bad cheese.

It was like a scene from a Dostoyevsky novel. I had been so fond of those books. I never imagined I would actually be living like a character in one.

The country remained almost completely shut down for weeks. Curfews were in force. Citizens were allowed out for a few hours at a time to buy necessities. Darkness meant you had to be inside — or else. The universities were closed. The courts were closed. Congress was shut down. Political parties were banned.

Everything was now ruled by the military junta, headed by Generalissimo Augusto Pinochet, who referred to himself as *El Jefe de la Junta*. The radio and TV stations were all controlled by him. The newspapers reflected what the government wanted them to reflect. Opposition papers were simply closed.

It was all so depressing for me. My father, however, had never been happier. He supported Pinochet. People needed to be killed to clean house, Dad said. It was the only way out for Chile.

Now the soldiers were everywhere in Santiago with machine

guns strapped over their shoulders. They watched everything from their positions in the streets and in the public buildings. The soldiers were usually drawn from the poorest classes, but they had real power now in this state of martial law. What was most unnerving was their policy of keeping the gun barrels trained on whoever moved near them. Their hands would automatically guide the eyes of the barrels to face you as you passed.

Little by little, the population began returning to normal life. People began returning to work except those whose names weren't on government lists and were deemed *personae non grata*. These people were summarily fired. On the other hand, those with connections to the military rulers were now quickly promoted. It was the new lay of the land. The reign of terror had begun.

College students were now on the outs. We were deemed major culprits who had supported Allende. At the end of October, the junta placed an ad in *El Mercurio*, the right-wing newspaper, urging every college student in the country in their last year of study to report to their campuses to see if they would be readmitted. I was to graduate in December. I doubted I would be allowed to do so now.

My father persuaded me to give it a shot. If I didn't show up to be readmitted, I would immediately be viewed as a leftist, he said. There was nothing on the records they could use against me, he promised. I hadn't been arrested. I had never planted a bomb in a government building. I had done nothing illegal, he said. Protesting in the streets was not breaking the law.

I finally listened to him. I built up my courage and showed up on a Monday outside the main entrance to the campus. There, in the subdued gathering of hundreds of students, were two of my best friends from school — Monica, who like me, was a member of MAPU, and Helga, a Socialist who had dated a boy in MIR. Corina, another friend and Socialist, did not show up. Her father had been a government employee. We three knew she was too afraid to come and that she may have been killed. Indeed, I don't know to this day if she is alive.

Monica and Helga, for their part, were very nervous. They were even uncomfortable being around me because of my connection to Michael. They told me they knew the CIA had been involved in the coup, and they also were certain CIA agents had taken photos of us at demonstrations. We didn't stand a chance of returning to school, they said.

Out of a history class of some 50 students who were to get degrees that December, six of us had appeared outside the main entrance to confront our futures. We stood there, quietly, with students from other classes. A command came over a loudspeaker that no one could talk. We readily obeyed; it was illegal now to form a group larger than three people in public.

We lined up to present our national identification cards to a military officer at the door. When it was my turn, I approached the entrance and produced my card. The officer filed it away and allowed me to proceed.

Soldiers at the door frisked me for arms. They ran their hands over my breasts and butt as many times as they liked. It was humiliating, but I just had to remain still and stoic, as if nothing was happening. The military had complete control of society, and made sure everyone knew it. Our spirits were completely crushed.

We students were directed to a room where we were made to sign documents stating our names and national identification numbers and a promise to not get involved in politics. We signed a statement that read, "I will only come to the university to attend my classes and when they are over I will immediately leave the premises and go home." The documents also made us swear we had not been part of the "rebel movement of Allende."

It was a bitter statement to sign, but what could I do with a machine gun in my face? You would sign or you might become one of *los desaparecidos* — the Disappeared. Some students and faculty had arrived before the university was officially reopened. A few of my own classmates had been shot. The soldiers had jailed one of my professors, Mario Céspedes, one of the foremost experts on Chilean history. Sr. Céspedes was a known

Allende supporter. We never saw him again.

I signed the documents. I promised I would be a perfect citizen.

"Come back tomorrow," I was told.

I returned every day for a week to see if I would be reinstated. But after that first day, I never saw Monica and Helga again and never learned what became of them. I phoned Helga's house once. No one answered. I did not pursue it. My father told me troops would be coming to search my house. I discarded all my books and tapes of national protest music, making sure nothing that could reveal my support of progressive causes remained. I hid my poems inside the pages of thick books. Years later, my mother came upon scraps of paper squirreled away in the strangest places.

Each day that I appeared at the university, a voice over the loudspeaker ran down the roll of majors. "Philosophy," it would read, then call out the names of several students who would be allowed in. When the voice came to, "History," only two people were ever named. I did not recognize these names; they were not part of my 1973 graduating class. I later learned that the two names belonged to students from years past who had never finished. They hadn't been on campus during the present volatile period, and so they qualified for reinstatement.

No one else in my class, it seemed, had clean records. I knew now that my name had appeared on some secret list. At that moment, I realized I would never finish my degree in Chile. My entire future seemed uncertain.

For his part, Michael was unsure whether he would be able to continue at CARE. We knew we had a decision to make. Actually, it seemed to have been made for us. In January 1974, we left Chile.

I was leaving in pain. I did not know what would be the fate of anyone close to me. I knew I would never see my friends again who had disappeared or were dead or had gone into exile, not only Corina and Monica and Helga, but also Guillermo and

María Cristina, from La Serena. What had become of them? This was not the Chile I had grown up in. It was now a country full of hatred and violence, torture, repression and despair. The thousands rounded up on September 11 had been herded into the National Stadium, the very arena where I had heard Allende and Castro speak so idealistically two years before. They were interrogated and tortured, and a number were shot. Many bodies were carried out.

My mother protested my decision to leave Chile. My brother had just died. Fortunately, my sister had returned from Venezuela. My mother would have at least one child near her. It was wrenching to say goodbye to them. My father also tried to talk me into staying. He was full of great plans. He assured me he could use connections with right-wing political parties to gain my readmission to school. I could get my life on track. My father saw Chile as a country on its way to recovery. For me, it was a country whose soul had died, and with its death went many of my dreams.

I was hardly excited to be heading to the United States. I spoke barely a word of English. It had always been my worst subject in school, and I hated it with a passion. The United States represented to me everything that I fought against. I viewed that nation as being responsible for killing Chileans. I was filled with disgust and dismay.

When I went to the U.S. embassy to get my permanent resident card ("green card," although it is blue), I was asked numerous questions: Have I ever been part of the Communist party? Was I going to engage in anti-government activities? These were the people who had just destroyed my country, and they were asking *me* if my intentions were to destroy theirs. I couldn't rid myself of the nagging ambivalence about coming to America. What on earth was I doing? But the die was cast, and there was no turning back.

I decided to see Latin America as I traveled north for my new life. It was a kind of therapy, a way to bring closure to this chapter in my life. My trip by train and bus through Latin

America proved a harsh lesson in geopolitics. My husband, the U.S. citizen, never encountered any trouble passing through customs, while I, the citizen of Chile, was viewed with deep suspicion.

We first went to Argentina to see my family. Grandma was still alive in Mendoza. I knew I would never see her again. I said goodbye to my aunts, uncles and cousins. Then we were off to Paraguay, Brazil, Bolivia and Peru. We flew from Ecuador to Panama, then traveled by land to Nicaragua, El Salvador, Costa Rica, Honduras and Guatemala. Central America proved especially difficult for my travel. The Americans were directed to a speedy customs and immigration line. The sight of my Chilean passport raised an immediate red flag, followed by questions.

"You want to become a political exile? Why are you leaving Chile? Are you escaping the regime? You are probably Communist."

In many countries, such as Costa Rica, I needed a special visa to be allowed in. My green (blue!) card helped; I was heading to the U.S., I would not be staying in their country. They need not worry about me. Indeed, the only country that ultimately refused me entrance was Mexico.

After we got to Guatemala City, we waited a month for my Mexican visa to come through. I only wanted to cross Mexico; I wasn't applying to stay for any length of time. Didn't they understand? I was made to go to the Chilean embassy. There, I was told I was on my own. The staff wouldn't help any Chilean citizens because so many were fleeing the country for political reasons.

At the Mexican embassy in Guatemala, it was as if I were back in Chile. I was made to sign documents stating I, Emma Sepúlveda, would not stay in Mexico, that I had not supported Allende, that I was not a communist, that I was not a rebel. Nonetheless, I never was allowed into Mexico.

We flew to Los Angeles from Guatemala City. Los Angeles was my introduction to the United States. After we landed and met Michael's friend, Bill, I was struck by the monstrosity of

concrete and freeways. L.A. was large, cold and insensitive —
everything I expected from the United States. The African-Americans kept to themselves, the Latinos kept to the Latinos, the
whites stayed with the whites. The whites drove the fancy cars.
The slums contrasted with the majestic high-rises. Clearly, there
was a great gulf between rich and poor.

That first night, some friends invited us to a Mexican restaurant to make me feel at home. They watched my face, believing
I was going to be thrilled to see food from home after traveling
so long. I opened the menu. My jaw fell.

Was this a joke?

Tacos? In Chile, "taco" means the heel of a shoe. Burros?
"Burro" means donkey. Could they be serious? I would never
eat donkey meat! I had not even been allowed to see Mexico,
and now these well-meaning people thought I was a Mexican. I
knew I had to keep a positive attitude and forge ahead.

Shortly after we arrived in Reno, I went to the state of Nevada employment office in search of prospects. I had an interview in Spanish, but the official who conducted the interview
only knew a few phrases in Spanish. After he reviewed my quali-
fications, he told Michael I had two choices: I could be a maid,
or I could be a dishwasher. How ironic — I hadn't even made
my own bed when I was growing up. I had the finest private
high school education and four-and-a-half years of college, yet I
was told that I was only qualified to start at menial labor.

America hardly seemed the "land of opportunity" at that
moment. I was no longer a privileged, educated young woman.
I was now an immigrant — dumb, dark and ignorant.

A Greenhorn, A Professor

IT WAS THE END of June 1974. Summer had arrived in Reno, in the dusty high-desert. I thought it was hell. We had come from the southern half of the hemisphere where it was winter. My body was not prepared for this drastic transition, and especially not for the humidity-free air of the Great Basin. I felt like my skin and my whole body was cracking. Nor was I ready for Reno itself. Santiago, with its smog, public transportation and crush of humanity, was an active, bustling city of four million people. It had been my life-long reference point for the definition of "city." But Reno was a small, rural town that proclaimed itself "The Biggest Little City in the World." It had barely 100,000 people. It seemed an outpost at the end of the world, and where practically everyone was white.

That was one of the first realities about Reno I absorbed. There were only one or two small areas of town where I could drive and encounter African-Americans. Latinos were relatively few. There were maybe one or two Mexican restaurants.

Everything was so white. Even the people looked like the desert. Their faces totally lacked color. Something of the surrounding sagebrush was in their constitution. They were like sagebrush — tough, growing obstinately in a harsh environment, without colorful bloom or lush foliage. Their manners and dress seemed so stiff and staid, much like the original pioneers and cowboys.

It appeared to me that these citizens went about their business stoically, disconnected from one another. The glaring exception to this mundane world was the handful of blocks in the middle of downtown, where casino neon flashed day and night, players smoked and drank and wagered non-stop, and female workers were scantily clad revealing the tops of their breasts and bottoms of their butts. Reno had a split personality.

My first venture inside one of these gambling madhouses was enough to dissuade me from returning. The clang and clamor of machines and lights and buzzers going off were cacophony, a garish and offensive sensory assault, a distortion of reality, submerged in a swirl of cigarette smoke and cocktail waitresses dispensing libations at a robotic pace. For an instant, standing there bewildered, time seemed to stand still. I was bathed in the artificial light of a netherworld whose occupants were passionately engaged in a willful escape.

Unlike everyone else in Reno, I walked everywhere. It was my only way of getting around, even in the July sun! We had a little apartment on Taylor Street, about a mile south of the University of Nevada campus, and perhaps a half-mile east of the downtown casino core. I walked through the sweltering heat to the supermarket as pickup trucks rumbled by. I yearned for a little four-cylinder car, a Fiat maybe, or a Citröen, to whiz past to remind me of Santiago. I couldn't get used to seeing people driving pickups with shotgun racks. They'd climb down from the trucks in cowboy boots, and I'd grow very nervous, wondering, "My God, are they going to start shooting each other?"

I knew next to nothing about Reno. I knew of its ultra-liberal marriage and divorce laws. My mental picture before arriving was that Reno was a mining town out of the Old West teeming with cowboys — a peculiar place. The television show *Bonanza*, set at nearby Lake Tahoe and on the Comstock, was very popular in Chile. I imagined I would encounter Hoss, Little Joe and the other Cartwrights. I had some dreamy idea that Virginia Street, the main drag, would be a sun-blanched boardwalk lined by saloons, where a cowboy would kick the swinging doors open and step out, six-shooters in holsters, to peer beneath the brim of his Stetson toward a road lined by horses and buckboards. Somewhere a tinny piano or a harmonica would be playing.

This reverie was not so far from wrong as one might think. I arrived eleven decades after Virginia City's mid-nineteenth century heyday. Virginia Street and all the other streets were paved, modern and full of cars. There was a small airport and a land-grant university, which was the center of what little cultural life existed. Reno was a gambling town; the economy depended on it. The city ebbed and flowed with the stream of gamblers and tourists coming east over the Sierra from California on the new Interstate 80. There was limited shopping with only one mall (Park Lane) and almost no fine restaurants and few apartment houses.

Overall, Reno seemed to me, at that time, to be white-faced, red-necked, and still reeking of leather. I felt like a Latina extra inserted into a movie script for comic relief.

There was the matter of finding a job. My interview at the state employment office had been horrifying. Fortunately, a friend of my husband had a wonderful idea to spare me from making beds or scrubbing pots for a living. He suggested that we check prospects at the Mexican restaurants. I was game for anything that would land me a job. It seemed only natural that I should seek a job that wouldn't require a knowledge of English.

Our friend and I walked into a Mexican restaurant on the main street in Reno. I didn't have a clue what my friend discussed with the woman at the cashier's stand, but suddenly a lovely man, very short, a bit pudgy, walked up with a big smile on his face and started speaking to me in very basic, broken Spanish. It was the language of someone who had very little formal education in Spanish. "You know, you're so cute that I think I have a job for you," he said. "You can be a hostess."

I had no clue what a hostess was. The man, the owner of the restaurant, didn't know the word for it in Spanish. He merely said, *"una hostess."* He explained that I had to smile a lot, greet people as they came into the restaurant and escort them to their table. I was as offended as when I had been asked to run for homecoming queen in college. I hadn't imagined that my looks would land me my first job in the United States.

The pay was around $1 an hour.

"Make sure not to take any tips, because the tips are for the waitress," he said, still smiling.

So I gave it a try.

In those years, the mini-skirt was in vogue. My hair went down my back past the hem. I had to wear big heels. I remember walking in on my first day with four phrases written on my hand: "Good evening"; "How many in your party?"; "Follow me"; and after I escorted patrons to their table and distributed menus "Have a nice dinner." I repeated these phrases hundreds of times that first day. If anybody said anything to me I just smiled, because I had no idea what they were saying.

It was a huge restaurant. As the hours went by I found my feet giving out, crammed as they were into unwieldy high heels. The cashier was a woman named Roberta. She spoke no Spanish, but communicated through a bilingual waitress. Roberta innocently asked if my feet were aching because it was the first time I'd worn shoes. Roberta had the idea people from South America normally went barefoot. It may have been a Mexican restaurant, but all the workers out front and in the bar were Anglos. The kitchen workers were from Mexico and Central America. From the first day, the cooks and dishwashers called me "*chingada*." I had no idea what *chingada* meant. I figured it referred to people from Chile.

On my second day, I was joined by a hostess who had started before me, 16-year-old Yolanda. She had been born in Mexico and spoke Spanish. "Oh, it's nice that you're going to be working here," she said. "We're going to be a pair of hostesses. What's your name?"

"Emma," I chirped, and added, proudly, "but you can call me *la chingada*." She started laughing so hard that I was embarrassed.

Then she told me that *chingada* meant fucker.

A few months later, I was standing in the kitchen of the restaurant getting a glass of water, when suddenly I heard screams of, "*La migra! La migra!*" In no time, the kitchen was empty.

My co-workers ran outside. I had no idea what was going on, so I ran, too. I didn't know what *"la migra"* meant; it wasn't a phrase we used in Chile. But in Chile there are many earthquakes, so the first thing that came to my mind in my desperation was that they must have felt an earthquake. Whatever it was, it was a major crisis. I knew I had to flee like everyone else.

Out the back door and into the parking lot behind Virginia Street we ran. Some of my co-workers got into cars and sped away. Others bolted down the street at top speed. I stood on the asphalt, anxious and perplexed, calling out, *"Qué pasa? Qué pasa?"* I was lost, and no one would explain to me what was going on. *"Corre!"* (run) they yelled. So I started running. Then I realized it would be smarter to drive. My keys were still inside the restaurant. I went inside. Roberta was still there and so were the people waiting on tables. The restaurant was not abandoned. What strange panic had gripped the others? Unfortunately, Yolanda, my security blanket, wasn't scheduled that day, so no one could explain to me what had just happened.

I hunted for my purse. Roberta asked me what was going on. *"La migra,"* I said, hastening to leave. "Emma, no," Roberta said, stopping me. She tried to explain to me why I didn't need to leave. She called another waitress over, one who had mastered basic Spanish to communicate with the cooks in the kitchen. *"Tarjeta verde, tarjeta verde* (green card, green card)," the waitress said. I told her that I didn't have any green card. She translated that for Roberta who looked at me and said, "Run fast, Emma." So, like a jackrabbit, I took off across the restaurant, in front of all the customers. As I was approaching the back door, the semi-bilingual waitress grabbed my arm and dragged me to where my purse was kept. I still didn't understand what was happening. She grabbed my purse, pulled out my wallet and went through it. She held up a blue immigration card and said, *"tarjeta verde* (green card)."

It was at that moment I realized how important that little card was. No matter what they called it or what its real color was, its lack kept undocumented workers — such as the kitchen

82

staff and busboys — in a constant state of apprehension. In addition, they were vulnerable to the pranks of co-workers who would sound the alarm of *"la migra"* to clear out half our work force.

I began to learn about the underground world of the undocumented workers, people who worked without the necessary papers. Sometimes one would want to return to their country to see family. So he would do something, perhaps commit a small crime, to cause immigration officials to detain and deport him. He would later return north, often leading a dozen or so friends. These workers never had qualms about telling me they didn't have their papers. Some couldn't read or write. When I was promoted from hostess to cashier, they would cash their paychecks and I would help them sign.

My boss, Miguel Ribera, was quite a character. His main claim to fame in Reno was that he'd arrived around 1960, with hardly a dime to his name but an incredible talent as a Mexican chef. He had bought his first restaurant with only $135 and faith in God, and ended up owning five.

He could see how miserable I was, going home in tears each night. He knew my goal was to finish school, but I would never be able to save the money for tuition earning menial wages. He decided that when the time was right he would pay for my tuition, books and health insurance.

But as I toiled along, all I felt was despair in my dashed ambitions that had been buried beneath the weight of expectations. I worked five or six days a week, sometimes seven when I could substitute for somebody. As an immigrant, I was immediately and painfully made aware of how people in my new land perceived me. My appearance invited two stock reactions from customers: "Look at this little Mexican, I wish I could take her home!" or "You're so stupid, why can't you communicate? What are you doing here if you can't speak the language?" Even my fellow native speakers took advantage of this. I had become, *"la chingada."*

There is a story from those days that I still tell my Spanish-language students. When you learn a language in a cursory course in high school — as I had learned a few words of English — you are never taught the dirty words. So I had never heard the foul words most Americans freely use. Indeed, I gamely struggled to serve the restaurant patrons as a perpetually smiling hostess, eager to please. When I would find myself adrift in a sea of incomprehensible English, I would do what non-lingo speakers do everywhere: I would guess at the meaning. After navigating enough close calls, a certain confidence develops.

I was a sponge, quickly picking up English through exposure by reading or watching television in my spare time. I began to lose my bashfulness. I started taking chances.

I should note that the restaurant's bar was an active sector of the establishment. The restaurant did a booming business in margaritas. After imbibing an unlimited amount, guests would sometimes reel from the bar to the dining room, to be guided by me to their seats.

Late one night, when I was still a hostess, an older woman made her way to the dining room entrance, barely balancing a large margarita glass, and asked for a table. I led her to a one with two chairs near the entrance to the kitchen. She looked at me and said, "I don't want this fucking table."

I didn't understand exactly what she was saying — no one had used this word with me before. But with my increasing confidence in my English, I quickly decided the adjective, "fucking" must mean, "close to the kitchen." Customers never liked to be seated next to the kitchen. So I merrily led her to a big table right in the middle of the restaurant, laid the menu beside her and asked loudly, with a big smile on my face, "Is this fucking table? Is this fucking table?"

The woman began screaming at me. The customers at the surrounding tables erupted in laughter. "Call in the manager!" the woman roared, red-faced. "Call in the manager!" She was making quite a scene.

Unfortunately for me, the owner was still at the restaurant that night. He rushed over. "*Qué dijiste?!*" he demanded. What did you say?!

"Well, I just asked her if this is a fucking table."

He could not believe it. "How could you possibly say that?" he exclaimed. "Punch out! Punch out!"

That was his standard response when he got pissed off at an employee. "Punch out." Take your time card, punch out on the time clock and go home.

Back in the kitchen, I was in tears. Everyone wanted to know what the *chingada* had said. "I said nothing," I told them. "I just asked this lady if that was a fucking table."

They couldn't believe it, either. "Emma, where did you learn that?" they said.

Finally, I said, "She told me first."

And so, though at great expense, I learned a new word in English. On the positive side, I now knew how to be insulting whether I was in Mexico or the United States.

One of the first things I did on arriving in Reno was to learn how to drive. I drove poorly, but with luck I had passed the driving test. I'd taken the written test in Spanish and practiced my driving weekend after weekend in the parking lot of Park Lane Mall, going round and round. It would take me forever to change gears in my tiny 1969 Toyota. I believe the language barrier actually helped me on my driving test. The instructor apparently took pity on me; whenever I could not perform a maneuver, he assumed I just hadn't understood his command, not that I couldn't execute what he had asked me to do.

This may have been a dubious achievement. Set legally loose on the streets, I would take corners in third gear, then the car would stall and I'd have to start it up again, impeding traffic. I drove so badly I was constantly given the "finger" by other motorists. In Chile, there is a far different hand sign used in such situations so that flashing the middle finger had no significance to me. Every time someone gave me the finger, I waved back with a big smile.

Despite my problems with English, I forced myself to do

the shopping. One day, I went to the local department store to buy bed sheets. I had seen the word "sheets" spelled out, but in Spanish this spelling would be written, "shit." So I translated this spelling to an English pronunciation, and asked the clerk for "shits." The clerk acted like this was the funniest thing she'd ever heard. She couldn't stop laughing. I was very upset. I kept repeating, "Yeah, I need shits." The other customers all were laughing, too. Finally I just apologized and left.

Incidentally, I never did correct my pronunciation of "sheet" even when I was a teacher's assistant at the University of Nevada in 1977 and instructed my students, "Okay, everybody take out a shit of paper." One of my students explained, "it's sheet." At that point I changed my instruction to, "Okay, everyone take out a piece of paper . . ."

The people of Reno in the 1970s had not been exposed to many people speaking other languages. If you didn't speak English, they believed you were stupid. I reflected that I had behaved the same way with regard to non-Spanish-speaking foreigners in Chile. American tourists seemed to be the dumbest creatures on the face of the earth, with their checkered Bermuda shorts, heavy shoes with white socks, ridiculous hats and faces burned by the South American sun. To top it off — they couldn't communicate with us.

I never dreamed that one day the tables would be turned.

My life in the United States was changing me, and slowly I began to realize that my husband and I had different ideas about what was important in life. Chile had thrown us together, now we simply grew apart. My political consciousness had been stirred deeply by the events of the past four years. I had only a partial understanding of what was going on in U.S. politics. My heart was still in Chile.

My conscience was haunted by the fate of my native country, and especially harrowed by the plight of *los desaparecidos* (the disappeared), those who had vanished suddenly and in most cases permanently in the wake of the political purge that followed the fall of Allende. A protest movement formed among the mothers and wives of the children and husbands who had been expunged by Pinochet's new regime. In quiet, even passive ways such as silent vigils and peaceful protests, these women pressed for information about the fates of their loved ones. My dreams kept taking me back to Chile to see what I could do to help them.

A few years earlier I had the dream that I will help save the world and now. . . I still believed I could. I wrote a letter to my family saying how miserable I was. I expressed my dislike of Reno and the fact that I was treated as a dumb Latina. Strangers would ask me what part of Mexico I was from. They all assumed I was from Mexico, and that I was an idiot. Even our friends' attitudes verged on condescension and indulgence, inquiring whether we drove cars in Chile. I grew so fed up that I decided I wanted to return to Santiago. My father sent me an airline ticket.

My trip to Chile changed my mind. I wasn't prepared for the shock. I knew things would be bad. I had read South American newspapers and had kept in contact with my conservative high school friends (having lost complete contact with my liberal college friends). I had gleaned bits and pieces of what was going on in Chile about the repression of the dictatorship. My mother had sent me magazines from Chile, but there was no longer any semblance of a free press.

I immediately realized that two years away from Chile had separated me from the misfortunes of my homeland. Now, at night in my mother's house, I had trouble sleeping because of the periodic machine-gun fire in the streets. There was a curfew. I had left a nation of prosperity and great personal liberties and had arrived in one where you couldn't go see a movie at night, or go to a discotheque or dine out with a friend. Everything would shut down at dusk and not reopen until the sun came up. I had returned to a country where the people were numb.

I woke with a start each morning, feeling desperate. "Mom, they're still killing people!" I'd say. She would be unmoved. She would tell me not to worry about the gunfire; the military was merely target-shooting. They fired into the air to impress citizens with the necessity to respect the curfew and to not leave their homes. "Oh, they're not killing anybody," she would say. "Go back to sleep. I'm used to it."

I quickly came to realize the gulf between the people who had stayed behind and those who had left. The ones who had stayed had generally come to accept the dictatorship and its violence as the only solution to "cleaning up" the country. They had no inclination to resist; they were entirely subdued. My mother, for example, gladly opened her purse for soldiers to search whenever she entered a public building. With no U.S. passport, just my green card to explain my U.S. residency, I had to carry my Chilean identification card with me wherever I went. And I could never get used to having to produce it on demand to soldiers.

My mother was very nervous because I was desperate to locate my college friends, Helga, Monica and Corina. "Forget it," she said. When my high school friends organized a little party for me, the guests had to arrive and leave at different times so that not too many people would be gathered in the same place. There was a limit to how many could meet together without government authorization, even for an afternoon tea!

I became so angry about these conditions that by the end of my six-week visit I was happy to leave. I was dying to return to the United States. When I landed at the airport in San Francisco, I felt I was back in my real home. Although there were many things about the United States I did not like or agree with, I knew I belonged here. The freedom, the protection I felt would never be the same anywhere else. In Chile, there was an army ready to violate citizens' rights. You could be shot if you went out your door at night, and during the day, you encountered stone-faced, helmeted soldiers with machine guns standing on every corner, the eyes of their gunbarrels following you. Whatever building you entered — the post office, the telephone company, the bank — you would be searched. I had felt the complete sense of being a prisoner in my own country, and I decided that jail wasn't for me.

My divorce from Chile was complete. I was now ready to move ahead with my life. While I considered that I would always face discrimination as an immigrant and a minority group member in the United States, I knew that I could overcome any discrimination in the "land of opportunity." On the other hand, it would be an impossible task to overcome the fear of death that I faced living in Chile.

The decision was made. My roots would be set down in Nevada. I would become a U.S. citizen. I vowed to become acceptable to America and to build a life there.

I earned my bachelor's degree in 1976 with the financial help of my boss at the restaurant. He knew I was unhappy being a hostess and cashier and that I dreamed of getting my degree. So after five months working at his restaurant, he granted me a "scholarship," paying for tuition and books.

"I think you can do it," he said. "Just prove to me that you can get the degree."

So I did.

On the strength of my previous studies in Chile, I was admitted to the University of Nevada as an undergraduate for the spring semester, 1975, which began in January. Fortunately, the admissions department granted me the maximum number of credits based on my five years of college in Chile. The courses I needed to complete a major in Spanish were a few literature classes plus the residency requirements — Nevada government, history and politics, and English.

I enrolled in a mandatory class, "English for Foreign Students." There were a handful of students from around the world: an African, a Japanese and a German. The Spanish-speakers consisted of a Colombian man, a Mexican woman and myself. It was a very small class, and the instructors spoke only English. None of us learned much. After that class, I took classes with the rest of the student body. Fortunately, my literature classes were in Spanish. I continued working at the restaurant, and also worked part-time in a campus job. I was on my way. I was part of America now.

In May 1976, I received my bachelor's degree. It had taken a year-and-a-half. My career path was clear to me now: I would become a professor. Latin American history had been my interest in Chile, but now, history was out. I always had a love of literature and so Latin American literature would be my field.

My knowledge of English had improved dramatically as I applied myself to the coursework, and I even garnered a number of awards for outstanding student in my Spanish classes. The foreign languages department accepted me into its master's program and gave me the opportunity to teach first-year Spanish. I gladly accepted. It was a small salary, but it meant I wouldn't have to pay graduate school tuition. I was able to quit work at the restaurant, where as a waitress I had earned enough money to buy a car.

By 1978 I had my master's degree and the university hired me as a lecturer. I was considered a fairly good teacher by now. I was proud to have made it to full-time professional employment without the aid of student loans. My old boss at the restaurant had given me a leg up at the outset — the rest had been up to me. Yes, I was making it in America. And fittingly, that same year, I became a U.S. citizen.

I read the required reading and went for an interview. I was asked a number of questions: How many stars are on the flag? Who was the first president? Was I going to become a communist? Did I have any intention of placing a bomb in a federal building? Did I intend to participate in drug trafficking or prostitution? I was tempted to tell the interviewer, "Hey, I don't know how the job market is going to be." I didn't, though. The man was dead serious.

My mother was visiting me at the time. She couldn't accept that I was giving up my Chilean citizenship. It was one of the most painful moments of my life. To her, my decision to accept U.S. citizenship was breaking a family tradition. Grandpa had emigrated to Argentina but he never gave up his Italian citizenship, my mother said. He died with his Italian passport clutched to his heart. My mother had lived her life in Chile as an immigrant, and she declared she would die with her Argentinean passport and a rosary held to her heart. Why, she asked, if I were raised with such a sense of pride and honor, would I give up something as meaningful as my Chilean citizenship?

My mother did attend the U.S. citizenship ceremony, which was held in a room at the federal courthouse. A small group of us were sworn in together. I still have the newspaper article with our picture. I raised my right hand and pledged to obey the laws and defend the country, all the while hearing sobbing in the background — it was my mother acting as though she were at a funeral. I too might've broken down and cried if it hadn't been for the presence of a young adopted Vietnamese girl standing next to me. This young girl also was being sworn in as a citizen, and I thought that if she, who had escaped a war, could withstand such an emotional moment, so could I.

Certainly, standing before the judge with my mother crying in the background, I felt like a traitor to my family. But then, hadn't I elected to give up my Argentinean citizenship for a Chilean one after I had turned eighteen? What's more, I knew if I were really going to be part of this new country that I wanted to live in, I had to be a citizen.

At the same time, I was wrestling with another emotion. I was afraid of abandoning my former culture. At eighteen, when I became a Chilean citizen, I hadn't experienced a significant cultural change, because Argentina is next-door to Chile. But becoming a U.S. citizen meant embracing a whole new way of life. There also were political questions for me. For example, I have always been a pacifist. Now I had to consider what my stance would be if America were engaged again in some foreign war? Then I started thinking about what the United States had done to Chile, destroying its democracy by supporting the military coup and General Pinochet. I didn't know if I could support such a foreign policy.

Many emotions coursed through me during that short ceremony. When it was over, I knew I had done the right thing. I had made a big, final decison and committed myself totally.

As a sideline to my Spanish studies, I took photography classes at the university. I made great progress and even had my own dark room at home. I was a serious photographer, and at one point considered making it my profession. But I had worked so hard to earn my master's in Spanish that I decided to relegate photography to a serious endeavor. Still, serious it was. I reached the stage where I began to show my work in galleries and at exhibitions. My photographs revealed my mourning over what had happened in Chile. My favorite subjects were churches and cemeteries. The subtleties and intricacies of their black-and-white shadings, their half-lit recesses and luminous arches reflected my own transitions. My pictures from my first trip to Europe in 1978 were almost entirely devoted to hand-tinted, 1930s-style depictions of the interiors of cathedrals and cemeteries.

Later, I traveled through Spain and Portugal, France, Greece and Italy, and made a pilgrimage to Sicily to see where my grandfather, Sylvestre Pulvirenti, had been born. I traveled alone. This solitude gave me time for introspection. I was searching for myself and for meaning, for some perspective from which I could understand my turbulent past.

My crisis was that I couldn't resolve my anger and anguish about the government oppression of the poor in Latin America. This anger was both a reflection of my past and of my current travels. During my travels in Mexico and Guatemala, I had viewed first-hand the abusive treatment of the native people in these countries. I devoted an entire exhibition, and later, a published book of photos, to Guatemalan Indian women. Their faces reflected pain, misery and defeat.

I realized that oppression was shared among many women throughout South American and not something unique to my life. In Guatemala I experienced some of the same feelings I had in Chile. I remember visiting a little town, Chichicastenengo, and walking in the market outside of a church when suddenly a group of soldiers came and attacked the Indians mercilessly, forcing them to leave the town. Tragically, the soldiers were Indians, too.

Later, I was taking photos of Indians being removed from a public bus (perhaps they had been sitting in the wrong seats) in Guatemala Antigua, the old city next to Guatemala City. A soldier came and took my camera and ripped the film out. It was so similar to the way the Chilean military had acted during and after the coup.

At about this same time, I realized that I could not escape feeling tremendous guilt over *los desaparecidos* — the disappeared victims of the military dictatorship in Chile. I felt terrible that while I was now living safely in America, other Chilean women had been taking incredible life and death risks to fight oppression. I was moved to reach out to help the women striving to find their lost husbands and sons, these mothers and wives who were now referred to as *arpilleristas* because they sewed tapestries, *arpilleras*, depicting the scenes of the purge, the arrests, interrogations and executions of their loved ones. The *arpilleristas*, with the aid of stalwart supporters, had smuggled these evocative pieces of art out of Chile, telling the women's story to the world and to raise funds to continue their struggle. I, too, longed to help them.

I wanted to return to Chile and help spirit their work to the world at large. But it would be a few years before I could join full time in this work. My own world was still too much in flux.

When I returned from another solo trip to Europe, two big decisions were finalized in my mind. First, I could not stay at the University of Nevada as a lecturer. Second, I could not remain in my marriage.

I moved into a little apartment on Plumas Street in Southwest Reno and filed for a legal separation, and for the first time in my life, I found myself living alone. My earlier feelings of alienation from Chile and later from the United States returned full force.

What was I doing in this country? I felt accepted by some

people but not by others. Some people, I thought, accepted me for all the wrong reasons. I was still cautious about airing my political views. I didn't want to antagonize anyone by discussing my experience in Chile and my convictions that the CIA had helped topple Allende. I was still ill at ease over whom I should vote for in elections, or if I should even be voting in this country.

I made my career move and accepted a fellowship to study for my doctorate in Spanish literature at the University of California at Davis, California. It was 1980. I had turned thirty — the age when you are supposed to have your life together. I had not yet obtained my sought-after Ph.D. degree. I had no family in this country to call my own, and everything I believed I knew and everyone I loved was thousands of miles away.

I was now completely on my own in the land I had adopted, though it seemed a land that hadn't adopted me.

Davis was a very clean, small, progressive college town with a street market and a large group of people very attuned to what was going on in Central America. This informed population was a most-welcome addition to my development after the conservative and isolated Reno community.

I immediately joined the students' Central American Political Action Committee on campus. Some fascinating speakers came to speak at UC Davis, including South African Archbishop Desmond Tutu, a key opponent of apartheid. The experiences in the Committee were my rebirth. The Committee helped refugees from political repression in Central America, providing them food and blankets as they took shelter in churches in Sacramento. From this experience I felt a growing solidarity with all Latinos. I was no longer an ex-Chilena; I was a Latina. I had rejoined the world. Davis was my home for five years.

In 1984, besides studying for my Ph.D., I devoted much time to my photography and poetry. On a lark, hoping just to win a new camera, I entered a national contest sponsored by Polaroid and Porsche. I was working with female nudes to produce an illustration for a book of poems by the late Juan Ramón Jiménez, the Nobel prize-winning Spanish poet. Out of 25,000 contest entries, I captured the top prize, a $50,000 special edition Porsche. I would have liked to keep the Porsche, but a poor graduate student attending a university on a fellowship could not afford the insurance on such a car. I sold it, but gained a lot of mileage from the attention. The news of my big win even reached Chile. Reporters called to interview this successful Chilena in the United States who had won such a big prize. For a few days I even considered forgoing my college career to be a full-time photographer.

Between 1980, when I moved to Davis, and 1986, when I finally finished my doctorate in 20th Century Spanish poetry, I flew between the United States and Chile a dozen times. My mission was to help *las arpilleristas*, who were working in the resistance movement against Pinochet. My skill as a photographer played an important role here. One of my best friends is a Chilean poet, Marjorie Agosín, who teaches at Wellesley College in Massachusetts. She called me with an idea. "I need you to fly to Chile with me to take pictures of these women who are working against the Pinochet regime. You know them. I know you've been involved with them already. Let's go together."

Marjorie knew I had been working with the "arpilleristas" after I had made a trip to Santiago to meet with the women who worked in the vicarage in Santiago. The Catholic Church was helping people who had suffered directly from the repressive measures of the dictatorship. The Church vicarage was an effective sanctuary. Someone chased in the streets by soldiers could race to the church doors and duck inside; the soldiers were not permitted by law to enter.

Marjorie and I met in Miami and took a plane to Chile. My name cleared the computer files in customs and I was free to leave the airport. I returned to the vicarage in Santiago. Some of the women there had been tortured, raped and jailed during the period since 1974. I took pictures of their work, but not their faces. They were making *arpilleras*, little patchworks that depict the scenes of repression in the country. The women asked us to take their artwork out of Chile. So Marjorie and I stowed them in our suitcases and brought them to the United States.

After working so closely with these women, I could never forget their stories. Years later, after my son, Jonathan, was born, my interest in their cause grew into an obsession. After his birth, I knew I could never live or die in peace were my son to ever "disappear." My work later bloomed into a book that recorded the testimonies of those powerful women *(We, Chile: Personal Testimonies of the Chilean Arpilleristas)*.

In Davis, I went full-steam to complete my Ph.D. The University of Nevada had an opening for an assistant professor of 20th Century Spanish Literature. Reno natives and longtime residents have a saying — "No one ever leaves for good. You always return to Reno." So it was with me.

In August 1986, I married again. My new husband, John, was from Reno and had just finished law school. It was his home town. As for me, Reno was where I had been born as an American. I, too, felt like Reno was home. I was invited to a conference on Spanish literature in Berlin, Germany, that John and I attended. At the time, I was three months pregnant. On our flight back from Germany, I became ill. I went to the hospital in Davis, where I lost the baby. The people at the hospital didn't know what went wrong. They performed a battery of blood tests. Finally, one of the tests came back showing an alarming count of antibodies. I was sent for more tests in San Francisco. It turned out I had lupus.

Lupus is a chronic disease in which one has an excess of antibodies in the bloodstream. Instead of attacking diseases, the antibodies fight one's own heart, liver, lungs and other organs. It is said to be hereditary. I remembered that one of my aunts died of lupus when she was thirty-five.

By the time I received this diagnosis, I was pregnant again. I faced a terrible choice: have an abortion, or risk a stillborn baby. I said I'd take a chance on motherhood, but the high risk factor of my pregnancy required me to spend the last four months of my term in and out of the hospital.

John, meanwhile, passed the bar examination for Nevada. We traveled back to Reno while I was pregnant and he began to practice law. I had accepted a position as an assistant professor at UNR; and then Jonathan Paul Steven Mulligan was born, fullterm and healthy.

One thing I refused to give up after moving back to Reno was political activism. I decided that if Davis was able to have a strong political community, then Reno could, too. I would join whoever was committed to making changes.

Reno had grown in the years since I had arrived in 1974. In 1978, the giant 2,001-room MGM Grand-Reno had been built, featuring what was then the world's largest casino. The MGM's appearance touched off a major casino and construction boom in Reno. A second mall came in, along with numerous subdivisions. And along with the increase of service-industry jobs came an influx of Latinos, especially from Central America and Mexico.

Now as I drove around town in 1987, I heard Spanish, saw Mexican markets and many more Latinos than there were before I'd left for Davis. More Latino students were enrolling at UNR. The community was gaining diversity.

I learned that Nevada Hispanic Services was the only area non-profit organization active in helping Latinos. NHS offered counseling and referrals for immigration, welfare, health care, housing and schooling problems. I soon joined the NHS board of directors. I saw it as my duty to reach out to my fellow Latinos. I knew I never wanted to be a "library professor," spending a career in academia teaching from just books. I wanted to give something back to the surrounding community thatwass paying my salary. I wanted my work to help the community practically.

Right off, I saw an opportunity to merge the need for practical speaking experience for my advanced Spanish students with the need for translators in the community. I created a class for students who had learned Spanish in the classroom to use their skills to help non-English-speakers in the community. Students from my class served as interpreters at hospitals, elementary and high schools, NHS, many non-profit organizations and the courts. Not only did these students gain hands-on speaking experience, but performed a real service to Latinos. These services helped the mother who'd brought her young child to a doctor and could not explain what was wrong with him, the patient at the diabetes center, who could now take advantage of booklets in Spanish; and the defendant who could now learn in the courtroom with what exactly he or she was charged.

The practicum course remains more important than ever. Reno's Latino population continues to grow, and now constitutes somewhere between 15 and 20 percent of the area population. Latino organizations have kept pace, and over the years I joined the boards of just about all of them. I also have founded a few organizations devoted to empowering the Latinos of northern Nevada.

If my diagnosis of lupus did anything positive, it was to spur me to pack as much life as possible into what years I have left. My activist work extended beyond the Latino community. I joined the boards of many other organizations. I knew I had been selected for some boards as a token Latina. But I also knew that the only way I would be able to educate people about the struggles of Latinos was to join their organizations. I also worked on numerous task forces to discuss the major issues affecting the Hispanic community.

Before I knew it, I was recognized as a Latina activist in Reno. I could now look back with pride on my twenty years in the United States.

My obligation to assist Chile in the people's struggle to return to democracy remained. My activities were no longer low-profile. Many university and social organizations knew I was helping the Chilean women. I was invited to speak at various universities and to many groups throughout the country. During the same period, I was hired as a consultant on the documentary film, *Threads of Hope*, narrated by Donald Sutherland. The film about *las arpilleristas* won a Peabody Award in 1993 and was nominated for an Emmy.

The international attention and the continuing work of the many people inside Chile have created a climate for change. Overall, Chile has made significant political reforms since the Pinochet regime came to power. In 1989, General Pinochet permitted a national plebiscite on whether the military government should relinquish control of the government. The result was a national vote that elected a Christian Democrat, Patricio Aylwin, president. Six years later, another Christian Democrat, Eduardo Frey, the son of the man who was ruling Chile when I campaigned for Allende, was elected to succeed Aylwin. However, Pinochet has remained behind the scenes, never far from public view or the reins of power.

Despite the return to democracy, *las arpilleristas* have never been able to get answers about what happened to their loved ones. A similar situation exists in Argentina, where a military reign of terror "disappeared" many of its citizens in the 1970s and 1980s during the so-called Dirty War.

Now it was 1994. My experiences with my family in Argentina and Chile, my new immigrant life in Reno, my political and academic life in Davis, and my community activism in Reno had prepared me for my decision to accept my citizenship fully. By that February night at Kyoto restaurant, I was on the verge of tossing my hat into the Nevada political ring. Were I to win a seat, it would provide a forum for me to publicly explore the issues I had grappled with on various community action boards.

I wanted to focus on four principal problems related to childcare, crime and education. I had seen that much of the crime, especially those committed against children, was related to the lack of affordable childcare in Reno. The backbone of Reno's economy was gambling. The bulk of the labor force were low-paid service workers, busboys and maids, cocktail waitresses and bartenders. What was needed was for the casinos to help their employees by providing affordable on-site childcare. I would work toward that goal.

The increase in crimes against children seemed the result of two circumstances. Parents often had to work at night. Children not only lacked supervision, but the parents would often return home tired and short-tempered. The stress of night work and no child supervision meant that the children bore the brunt of parental anger and accidents due to neglect. The existing Nevada statutes inadequately protected the rights of children. Abused kids ended up in the social system and were all too often returned to their homes only to suffer more abuse.

I started with the assumption that much of the problem could be resolved if the community could increase affordable childcare. The current statistics on child abuse were alarming. Nevada led the country in the proportion of children under age five who died at the hands of their parents.

The second problem I could identify was the increasing rate of crime and incarceration. Nevada has the nation's highest incarceration rate. Public officials and politicians seemed primarily interested in how to build more prisons and jails. But I was more concerned about crime prevention. It struck me as strange that drug addicts were continually put behind bars, where little or no treatment existed to help them overcome their problems, while violent offenders would win parole because the correctional system was under intense pressure to release prisoners until more prison beds could be provided.

The third problem I saw was the low level of education among the population. Nevada ranks high among the worst of the fifty states in college attendance after high school. As an educator, I was shocked to learn that the high school dropout rate practically led the nation, and as for those who completed their first twelve years of school, fully 70 percent made no effort to seek post-secondary education. I hoped that the state could provide more options for post-secondary study that would provide our citizens with more technical and professional training.

The fourth problem was campaign finance reform. Campaigns have become a very expensive undertaking. Only the rich or those who could raise money from the rich would thrive in our current system. Campaign reform was needed to provide the voters with information about the source of a candidate's funds. I favored full disclosure of campaign donors and how the money was spent.

I also knew I had to be crystal clear on two hotly debated issues on which many voters wanted to know where I stood — abortion and capital punishment. I would not compromise when it came to the issue of abortion. My experience in high school with my close friend had fixed my stance for good. I would never agree to let government interfere with the right of a woman to have a legal and safe termination of her pregnancy.

I was not so certain about the death penalty. I had seen the corpses floating in the Mapocho River after the fall of Allende. I had seen what had happened under Pinochet's dictatorship and other tyrants in Latin America — the executions of political prisoners without a trial. However, after one of my dear friends was senselessly killed in Reno by a young white supremacist, I rethought my position.

My murdered friend had been an office manager for a medical group. More importantly, he was gay. He was stabbed 29 times in an empty high school parking lot late one Saturday night after he had agreed to give his assailant a ride home from a park. It had been a set-up. The young neo-Nazi, goaded by his peers, had been out trolling for a homosexual victim. The assailant, now serving a life term without the possibility of parole, had intended to carve a swastika in my friend's body but didn't have enough time. The assailant took the victim's car keys to ensure that the stabbed man would not be able to get help. I reconsidered my position and determined that from then on I would support the death penalty.

The four issues of childcare, crime-prevention, education and campaign finance reform became the crux of my platform. Later, as I committed them to print in my campaign literature, some powerful people attempted to have me modify them. I remember the remark of one female politician, who had read my brochure and commented, "Why are you concerned about child abuse? Children don't vote."

My answer was because children are vulnerable. It was at the center of what led me to this country and my decision to seek public office. I remembered my young brothers and the thousands of other vulnerable people who died because of the chaos in Chile. I knew that any community unable to protect its children could not claim a future.

The Circus Begins

PLOTTING A SERIOUS RUN in a primary race at the county or state level, even in a small state like Nevada, means assembling a tightly knit, dedicated and finely honed campaign machine. The stakes seem so high that you want a political consultant. Organization, strategy and tactics are everything. Much energy is necessary to craft the best possible media image, to prepare mailings and a blitz of bumper stickers, signs and brochures; to buy the right kind of advertising on radio and television; to map out precise walking routes for door-to-door canvassing.

My first item of business before officially filing for the Democratic primary for state Senate, District 4, was to assemble a core group of dedicated volunteers. These were friends and political activists who knew more than I did about running a campaign. The activists weren't too difficult to recruit. When a major-party candidate tosses his or her hat into the ring for a big race, the word spreads quickly in political circles and activists turn out to help. The first serious meeting of the Committee to Elect Emma, on a Thursday night, was packed. State senators and assembly members from Las Vegas and Reno along with Democratic party officials attended. About forty people jammed my living room. The house hummed with energy and enthusiasm.

We were going to win!!

The din of chatter among the beer-swigging, pretzel-chomping throng suddenly stopped. Assemblywoman Jan Evans strode up to the front of the room and eyed the gathering. She smiled a practiced politician's grin conveying confidence and control and said, "I'd like to introduce to all of you my long-time friend, someone I have unconditional support for, the next senator from District 4 — Emma Sepúlveda!"

My God! Far from buoying my spirits, Jan's enthusiastic introduction only tightened the knot in my stomach. Every time I heard those words during the following weeks and months, my doubts about having the strength it takes to run a political campaign boiled to the surface.

I had little time for introspection, though. Immediately after Jan introduced me, claps, yelps and whistles filled the room. The sounds then subsided like a wave. All heads turned toward me. I froze. I wanted to leave the room and flee into my bedroom. Here I was, a woman who daily spoke in front of a class full of bright college students. Now, my poise in public abandoned me. I didn't know what to say. At the same time, I sensed the need to charm everyone — the burden of being thrust into the spotlight.

Out of the corner of my eye I caught Jan Evans and Dina Titus, State senator from Las Vegas: two strong, politically savvy women. I could feel their eyes on me, along with everyone else's. I knew I had to force myself to talk. The moment of truth had arrived, even if I were entirely unprepared and even if I weren't sure what was going to come out of my mouth.

I remembered my father's speeches and recalled the tremendous confidence he conveyed each time he spoke. His speeches had been in his native tongue while I had to learn to give speeches in my second language. Gripped with self-doubt, I began to speak. My voice sounded high and weak. I started by explaining the novelty of this experience. "I feel very much like a novice," I said quietly. "But I will do the best I can, and certainly be there for everybody." I promised I would work hard. I said I really hoped I would win and become their senator.

It was a very short speech, and not what I had wanted to say. The applause I heard was certainly a relief, but I barely heard it. My mind was racing. What if I were to stand suddenly, thank everyone for coming, and declare, "I'm extremely sorry, but I'm not going through with this. I am scared."

Didn't these people realize that by entering small state politics, where political clout is in the hands of a few powerful people, my family or I could really be hurt, perhaps my career ruined? I discovered at that moment that speaking as a professor is entirely different from speaking as a politician. The professor is the expert, the star, in control of the situation, and the politician is the servant, the representative voice, at the mercy of the constituents.

As I talked about political issues, I did so with the knowledge that most of the people in my living room probably knew more than I did about many of the issues. What's more, I was not teaching them; I was persuading them to both support and vote for me. I was telling them, "I'm the best and you should support me because I'm the one who can most fully represent you." At the same time I realized that I had to be myself. My political "style" would show people who I really was. I knew I couldn't put on an act to impress them or fool them.

Other people were speaking now. "What is the most important thing to winning a campaign?" the activist Jan Gilbert said.

"Money!" another said.

"Let's start right here," someone else said.

Immediately, checkbooks popped out. We raised $1,500 on the spot.

That night, the first woman ever to run for the U.S. Senate in Nevada, Maya Miller, took me aside and told me my campaign would prove whether a female minority member stood a chance in state elections. "This will be the acid test for politics in Nevada," she said (and I will never forget that as long as I live!). Maya became one of the biggest emotional and financial supporters of my campaign.

That first meeting provided the human element for my campaign. I couldn't enlist everyone into my "kitchen cabinet." Those who were veterans from previous races counseled that it was better to have a small group planning and managing the campaign and to use everyone else for the grassroots work, walking the district.

Despite my misgivings and self-doubt, I began to gain confidence. It was certainly an impressive group. Its members represented the voices and views of an array of ethnic and religious groups, labor and business interests, students, seniors, gays and straights. I thought that my campaign was special because I could bring such a diverse group together. They were people ready, willing and able to commit seventy hours a week to the campaign if needed. Some of them were battle-hardened from prior campaigns. Their experience would prove indispensable in the fight ahead.

My core group was composed of idealists as well as realists; dreamers as well as doers. My "kitchen cabinet" included a long-time lobbyist for Nevada women voter groups, a former state Senate candidate, a veteran environmentalist, a gay activist, and a founder of the new group, PLAN, dedicated to electing progressive candidates to political office. There was a state lobbyist who had worked on every bill of significance for Native Americans. The group also included Yolanda, my old friend from the Mexican restaurant who had gone on to a banking career and had risen to be the first Latina woman to head the Department of Taxation in Nevada. There was a woman who worked in community development for the city of Reno and other individuals who had worked in the office for Nevada Hispanic Services. From that office came our computer expert: Yolanda Ortíz. The group's lawyer, a woman member of a prestigious Reno law firm, was in charge of keeping us in compliance with the vagaries of election laws.

We had the resources of land developers, lawyers, teachers and some of the best artists in our state, several university professors, some union leaders, and a few African-American woman leaders. My husband, John, took charge of the fund-raising committee. Rounding out the kitchen cabinet was Pamela Driggs, a dear friend from college and the daughter of the former chairman of the university's political science department. If there was one person who represented complete sacrifice for this campaign, it was Pam. She had quit her teaching job at a private school in Arizona and moved to Reno to help run my campaign.

To have so many competent, accomplished, respected and caring people team up for my election gave me new-found strength and willpower. It was not *my* campaign. It was *our* campaign. I asked myself, "Why have these fine people selected me to represent them?" My answer was that I was a new voice, a voice that had never been heard as a state senator in Carson City. I was a member of an ethnic minority group, a woman, an immigrant. I represented the millions of others who had come to pursue the American Dream. I was a common person in touch with the social issues that concern the working man and woman. I could be the desired citizen-legislator.

But I also knew that partisan interests motivated these supporters. Some had come to attain the same policies I pursued. Some came because working together to achieve a common goal provided a sense of solidarity. Some hoped that I could win the prize of unseating the Republican senator for District 4 and giving the Democrats an 11-10 majority in the Senate.

My political campaign also attracted an army of bright-faced volunteers. The biggest surprise were the numbers of strangers who showed up out of nowhere, declaring they were ready and willing to work on my campaign. Among them were senior citizens, university students, high school students, casino workers, writers, artists and many Latinos. Their work honored me, and we needed every body we could get.

At first, the "kitchen cabinet" engaged in weekly planning meetings. Later, after we established the routines of our campaign apparatus, we shifted into a higher gear — walking the precincts and knocking on thousands of doors. It soon became inescapably clear to me that a campaign is a complex, all-consuming enterprise demanding the logistics of a military operation and the endurance of an athlete. A campaign, any campaign, is simply hard, exhausting work.

After that first committee meeting we had three months to raise funds, place signs, organize coffees, arrange for me to appear at breakfasts and luncheons for many organizations and special-interest groups, attend candidates' forums, achieve name recognition with the voters, and make a big showing in the September primary election. I couldn't sleep at all the night after that first meeting, nor for many more nights to come.

The mixture of emotions, the optimism and the panic fueled my insomnia. Up until a few days before my decision to run, I had not realized that a state Senate race in a small district with 29,000 registered voters would be so intense. But here I was, with the firm knot in my stomach as a fixed reminder that there was no turning back, no backing out.

People who dismiss running for office as a massive ego trip have little idea what an ordeal a campaign is. While it may be foolish to run for public office in these times, the treachery lies not in the campaign, but in the terrifying encounters with some citizens. Every morning for the next five months, I rose with that knot in my stomach and a foreboding of what might happen to me that day. Who was going to attack me publicly? What was going to be printed in the newspaper? I felt apprehensive when I saw how a political campaign quickly outgrows the person who is running for office and takes on a life of its own. Every minute of my existence for the next five months would belong to this campaign. My days were planned down to the hour. I had no personal life anymore.

Deep in my heart I knew that if everybody pulled together for the duration of the campaign and if we all did our jobs — we would win.

The committee to elect Emma met initially for two hours each Thursday evening. We gathered at my house until a lawyer who supported my campaign gave us the entire third floor of an office building for our campaign headquarters. Our main goal at the outset was to organize a giant kick-off campaign bash/fundraiser. At the same time, the most pressing item of business for me was finding a political consultant to mastermind my campaign. The task of finding such a consultant was far more difficult and frustrating than I had imagined.

The campaign specialist would be critical to my campaign. He would put in place an election plan, research the opposition, organize my media campaign (the advertising buys and sound bites), orchestrate our tactics for the heat of battle, and coordinate the work of simply getting out the vote. We in the "kitchen cabinet" knew all too well that the race would likely be the fiercest fought in the state that year. My confidant, Asemblywoman Evans, did not downplay the opposition's ruthless willingness to distort my character and policies, and to block my access to contributors. She had no illusions about how the opposition would attack. They would try to characterize me as a bleeding-heart liberal, or a flaming radical bent on raising taxes and showering entitlements upon the disenfranchised. And that was just for starters. They would not let me or the public forget that I was not a native-born citizen. After all, it was 1994 and everyone was taking a shot at immigrants, blaming the non-native born for all the ills of our society.

She also knew the opposition would move quickly to block access to the big campaign contributors. Some of my key aides quietly confided to me that I'd never be able to raise enough money to win. I didn't believe them. I optimistically insisted we could prove to be more resourceful than anyone had imagined. Little did I realize that the blocked access would begin with my hunt for a consultant.

My search began locally. I needed a consultant who knew local and state politics. I developed an A list and a B list of possible consultant candidates. The A list included people who had run other campaigns or actually run for office, and whom I had seen in action. A pattern of interaction soon developed. I would meet with a person in some secret place. The person would be willing to help me and be excited about running my campaign. He or she would indicate that I stood a decent chance of winning. A few days later, the consultant candidate would call back and tell me that something had come up and that he could not run my campaign.

After the third time this pattern of initial acceptance and then rejection emerged, I asked a women I knew to run my campaign. I had worked long hours on her first campaign for the Reno City Council. After she initially said yes, she later stopped by my house and said, "I would love to run your campaign. I have great admiration for you. I think you would be wonderful. But I cannot do it." With her voice rising, she explained that she was opening a business in Las Vegas and it would consume too much of her time to allow her to manage my campaign. She also advised me not to run. She left my door wiping away her tears. I was dejected. I needed to talk to someone so I phoned Jan Evans.

She said only one thing: "They got to her."

My B list of candidates included people whom I knew were smart and capable and could handle my campaign, even if they hadn't run an entire election effort before. One was a friend who owned a local advertising agency. She had handled the media portion of other campaigns. She was very willing to help me. I felt a weight lift from my shoulders. When I took the news to my committee, I learned she would not be the right choice. Veterans of political wars in my inner circle reminded me that I could be sacrificing the political future of whomever I hired. "Be very careful now not to bury somebody," one wise aide said, "because your campaign is going to be extremely hard, and there are a lot of people with a lot of power in this state who will make sure that whoever helps you now will pay for it later on."

That fixed my decision. I would have to look outside the state for a consultant.

As eager as I was to locate a political consultant, I vowed I wouldn't settle for just anyone with a track record. I needed a consultant who would work with my style, who wouldn't try to remake my image. I didn't want someone who would insist I cut my hair, change my accent, and switch to "pro-life" policies. I didn't want an image tailor. I needed someone personable, who believed in my cause, and who knew what it would take for an immigrant Latina woman to win office in the United States in the 1990s. Specifically, I needed someone who understood that the electorate expects stylistic differences between men and women candidates. I also needed someone savvy about producing political advertisements since so much of my budget would go to buying television time. I also required someone who was strong in opposition research because I was running against an entrenched incumbent.

I wanted a consultant who was a Democrat. I did not think that a consultant could fully involve himself or herself without an emotional commitment to the same party as the candidate. For me, the Democratic party is the party of the people. It is concerned with the needs of the working class, women's issues, minority rights, better education, a fairer distribution of wealth, and moderating the tax burden on the middle class. I would have a Democratic political consultant even if my search was too time-consuming. I came perilously close to running out of time.

I deliberated with the senator from Las Vegas, Dina Titus, and with Jan Evans. We finally decided it would be best to pool my resources with several Democrats running for the state Legislature and to hire a more expensive consultant who would come to Nevada and direct multiple races. I would get his services half the time; the remainder would be divided up among, perhaps, three Assembly-seekers.

It was the beginning of June. We were a month away from our big kickoff campaign party. I was feeling the pressure. Another Las Vegas senator gave me the name of a consultant from a San Francisco law firm. The senator flew up from Las Vegas and the three of us met secretly in a dark bar at a local hotel-casino. The political consultant candidate was about thirty-five, aggressive and sharp. He had a quick wit, keen intelligence and was confident and energetic. "I love races like this," he said. "I think I could really make it happen for you."

We talked awhile. I liked him. He had tremendous experience. He had a very impressive résumé with recent work running various candidate campaigns all over California as well as directing ballot proposition drives. Yet, throughout our discussions, he kept calling me Dr. Sepúlveda or Professor Sepúlveda. I knew he regarded me more as an intellectual than as a politician. Furthermore, he told me he needed $5,000 a month salary. That amount was far from my expected budget with only a stream of $5 and $10 checks dribbling in!

I was such a neophyte that I hadn't realized that political consulting was so expensive. I had not imagined raising money merely to pay my "consultant." I was not aware that electoral politics was such a thriving industry. My political greenness was graying fast.

A few days later, a reporter with the *Las Vegas Sun* called me. He asked if I were going to hire this candidate as my consultant. He told me that the candidate had represented the Culinary Union in Las Vegas. Apparently our "secret" meeting with the candidate had not been so secure. I told the reporter from the *Sun* that I had met with the consultant only one time and that I was interviewing a number of other people but had signed a contract with no one.

That same day I got a call from a large consulting firm in Washington, D.C. The person I spoke to said that the word was out through the Democratic hierarchy in Las Vegas that a candidate in a tough Reno district race needed an out-of-state consultant to handle her election. He offered his services to be my media adviser. What intrigued me was that his firm was doing political consulting work in Colombia, South America. I was tempted to hire him, but I knew I didn't want to divide my consulting needs among more than one person. One person was expensive enough.

I became tired of looking. I told my committee I intended to run my own campaign. They told me in no uncertain terms that this was too important a race and that I was too inexperienced at running a campaign. They reminded me that I would barely have enough time to meet the voters.

Soon after, I received another phone call. It was from a consultant in Arizona who had worked on the get-out-the-vote effort in connection with the recent campaign of one of Nevada's U.S. Senators. This consultant flew up from Phoenix and Dina Titus flew up from Las Vegas to meet with me. We met early in the morning at an out-of-view corner table in a local restaurant across from the airport.

These clandestine meetings always made me uneasy, as though I were operating slightly out of the purview of the law. What was the big deal? I was hardly a familiar face in the community (at least, not yet). I didn't like arriving at 7 a.m., skulking to a remote corner table and taking several trips to the restroom as I waited for my contacts to show up.

The consultant from Phoenix, David Steel , had worked for Arizona's U.S. Senator, Dennis DeConcini, in Washington, D.C. David was a go-getter in his mid-to-late thirties, very preppy in his blue blazer and gray pants. I didn't take to him at first. When I said I intended to canvass door-to-door in my district, it surprised him. "You wanna walk?" he said. He didn't know Nevada that well but at the same time I felt I could learn a lot from this man. He seemed down-to-earth and I sensed he knew a great deal about how to get campaigns off the ground. He was a rainmaker. He knew how the political machine works, who calls the shots, what the role of the lobbyist is, and what a candidate must do to get the most out of those lobbyists. David also was a Democrat. He believed strongly in the same issues I did, and he was aware I wasn't going to alter my image or platform.

I began to see I could work with him, that he would give me enough space to be myself. At the same time, he agreed to work for a number of candidates. He would serve as a consultant for my race and three other Assembly races with women candidates. Also, he was "affordable." That is, if contributions came in as expected I could cover my portion of his salary.

Not everyone in my committee was pleased. Some believed that David didn't know what it would take to beat an incumbent at the state level. Some were concerned that David relied too much on money to win, which just didn't fit the grassroots flavor of our effort. But mine was always the final say in the committee. I hired him.

David flew to Reno two days later. The Committee to Elect Emma had to devise our campaign theme.

I was slowly but surely learning my district, driving its streets almost daily in my spare time and marking out on a yellow legal pad where my campaign signs should go. The geographical boundaries of District 4 are uneven. The District boundaries had been redrawn the year before to ensure parity in the number of voters with other districts. To accomplish this redistricting, outlying neighborhood pockets were added to the original sections inside Reno.

The differences among the sections of the district ran deep politically, economically and socially. District 4 includes Hidden Valley, an upscale suburban neighborhood spread along the eastern foothills of the Virginia Range, with two golf courses. Into this neighborhood, wild horses descend in winter to forage in homeowners' front yards, occasionally to be chased through the streets by irate residents in golf carts. At the other end of the socioeconomic spectrum is the Neil Road/Peckham Lane neighborhood in southeast Reno. A large number of recently arrived Latinos and other low-income people live here. Many of the families are crowded into one-bedroom apartments. District 4 also includes the established, tree-lined, brick-home blocks of Reno's Old Southwest ("old" meaning pre-1950s housing; "south" meaning south of the Truckee River that cuts through downtown; and "west" meaning west of Virginia Street, the main street stretching the length of town). These blocks of the Old Southwest include middle-class professionals and up-and-coming families living in old Victorian homes. Old Democrats live next to New Republicans. Moving farther south, District 4 grows more affluent and more conservative, like Hidden Valley.

The district map impressed me with how cumbersome campaigning door-to-door would be. Traveling through each street within the District boundaries opened my eyes to the town's layout. When I wasn't making hundreds of phone calls to lobbyists, organizations and people to learn more about their concerns, I would walk through the district's streets. It struck me that so much of the terrain was unfamiliar to me, even though I had lived in Reno for 20 years. To think I could end up representing this varied constituency gave me a feeling of tremendous responsibility. I told myself, "This will be the greatest challenge of my life, to be able to be the senator of all the people."

As an immigrant, I could relate to the Neil Road/Peckham Lane residents more than anybody else who was running in our community. I had lived in a New Southwest Reno apartment and now I lived in a nice home in a good area. I could relate to the people in these neighborhoods as well. I thought I could represent especially well those in need of assistance. To paraphrase President Clinton, "I feel their pain." Since I understood the needs of both the rich and the poor of the district, I knew I belonged to District 4.

What's more, I believed my opponent had never toured these streets as I now had. If he had, he would never have voted the way he did on key issues. For example, he had moved to salvage the State Industrial Insurance System by making it more difficult for injured workers to gain their rightful benefits under the state-mandated worker compensation system. He would not have cut cash benefit funding, reduced the money for retraining, or eliminated choices of physicians had he visited with voters whose lives had been turned upside down by an accident at work. The working-class neighborhoods in District 4 deserved better.

My opponent had voted against the Women, Infant and Children Program bill that funded more food for mothers and infants below the poverty level. My opponent had also voted against class-size reduction in elementary schools. I visited schools in lower-income areas of the district where there were as many as 35 students in a classroom. Was he entirely oblivious to conditions in his district's schools? I was beginning to see why so many people wanted my opponent unseated. I settled on my campaign theme: "A voice of integrity and commitment for the community."

The June deadline to file for the September primary election passed. I had no opponent in my party's primary. My opponent did. All the rumors that had filtered into our committee meetings proved false, including that the Republicans were going to recruit someone to challenge me on the Democratic ticket. The incumbent Republican, meanwhile, had to face a city bus driver in the primary where the main issue would be the incumbent's handling of SIIS reform.

Our committee viewed all this with delight. If a member of his own party had the guts to challenge him, surely that indicated he could be taken. The fact I was running unopposed meant I had a bye for the primary election, and I needn't worry about dividing my base support.

The time had come to start posting my campaign signs. The Committee to Elect Emma deliberated over what our signs would look like. We discussed colors and images. Through it all, I was adamant about what I wanted. This may seem like a trivial matter, but it wasn't to me. Every element that stamps one's name in the minds of the voting public is crucial in a campaign. And that includes campaign posters.

A very distinct picture of my posters was in my mind. My first name would appear bigger than my last name. I was to be the candidate of the people. The colors I envisioned for the signs were Nevada sky-blue and bright yellow — the hue of the rising sun to symbolize my campaign. My signs would incorporate a representation of my heritage, the evocation of a new beginning, and a brilliancy of color that would stand out in the sea of other campaign signs. The sun would play prominently in the design. For Latin Americans, the sun symbolizes light, new life, new beginnings. I placed this sun against the backdrop of the high-desert sky I had fallen in love with. I have always drawn inspiration from this Nevada sky. I have found that even on the grayest, snowiest winter day, at some point of the day this blue sky was sure to present itself. Finally, "Emma" was fixed prominently on the signs. My first name would convey that I sought to be approachable, to be close to the people I would be representing.

My committee members advised that it would be a mistake to put a party affiliation on the sign because people in Nevada tend to vote for the person and not the party. So the final addition of "Senate 4" in yellow letters under "Sepúlveda" completed the design. My signs stood out among the hundreds of other campaign placards plastered everywhere in the district. My signs were bright and hopeful, not too ethnic, not too staid, and attractive to passing motorists.

My opponent, meanwhile, spared no expense advertising himself. He placed a large billboard on the major intersection of South Virginia Street and Moana Lane. The sign faced me as I drove to work. Every morning I was greeted by his larger-than-life image. The billboard contained only his name. There was no mention of the district he represented, no plea for the people's votes — just, "Senator. . . ."

The grunt work of assembling 2,000 campaign signs and posting them around town fell largely upon my family. I'd rise early in the morning and go right to the garage to begin fastening the weather-proof, printed plastic sheets to the steel stakes with plastic clips. My hands became raw and filled with cuts. If putting the signs together wasn't taxing enough, posting them also proved an ordeal. On weekends, John would load up a new pile of 4' x 6' foot signs into the back of the pickup, then off he'd go. He'd put the big signs on streetcorners and in vacant lots. On weekday evenings, Cristina and I would load our smaller signs in that half-ton pickup, then motor off to make our door-to-door rounds. I had never driven a pickup in my life. It was like wrestling a mighty beast to obey my commands. When I sat in the driver's seat I could barely see above the steering wheel. Backing it up was almost impossible. Parking could only be accomplished if there were at least three spaces available, and then

I would end up several feet from the curb.

Cristina and I pounded the pavement doing door-to-door campaigning. At those golden addresses where we'd receive positive feedback, we'd inquire whether we could put a sign in the yard. We would record the affirmatives on a notepad, then just before sundown we'd return to each of these addresses. We also had a list of people who had called our campaign headquarters and requested a sign. One of us would hold the post straight while the other clobbered it with a large hammer. I relished this about as much as having a tooth drilled. The inevitable slips, scrapes and smashed fingers only added to our misery. Cristina and I became quite adept at swearing in Spanish and quick to change our pained faces for a smile whenever someone peeked through the window at us. The act of wielding the heavy hammer and ramming down a steel rod into unyielding sod took more strength than I could muster without extreme effort. I quickly reached the point where I beseeched people to water their lawns to make it easier for me. Any romantic notion about conducting a grass-roots campaign evaporated on our first night of sign-posting.

Typically, my night wasn't over after Cristina and I finished our sign-posting rounds. Instead of retiring to a hot bath and warm bed, I'd stop by campaign headquarters to sign hundreds of letters — thank you missives or requests for money or support. But this campaign was not solely a family affair. The Committee to Elect Emma had the troops well coordinated. About 20 people staffed headquarters on weekends. Dozens more would show up Saturdays for massive canvassing of neighborhoods, walking en masse to knock on doors, leaving brochures and putting up signs. My campaign, however, wasn't only waged in the trenches at the grassroots level. As a candidate in a key state race, I had begun to receive support at the highest levels of the Democratic party.

At the beginning of May, right before I filed, a woman who worked in U.S. Sen. Harry Reid's Reno office, Anita Sullivan, called me. She said the senator was flying to Reno and wanted to meet me and discuss my campaign and learn about my issues. I was thrilled. If there was one elected official I admired in Nevada, it was Harry Reid. In my opinion he had integrity. I'd heard him speak not only on television but in person at organizational meetings and social gatherings. He was more than just a polished politician; he had the courage of his convictions. I looked forward to meeting him, but I also was very nervous. What sort of impression would I make on him? Would I be able to get his support?

Of all places, he asked me to meet him at the airport because there are special VIP meeting rooms there. I arrived an hour early. I didn't want to be late, but I couldn't find the office! I hiked in my high heels up and down the stairs outside the airport administrative suites. I asked everyone I saw — administrative staff, security guards, airport travelers — if they knew where the meeting rooms were. Nobody could help me. This is it, I thought. One of the most important meetings of my life, and I can't even find the room! I had been too casual when his aide had phoned, not bothering to take down explicit notes on the location. I figured I'd show up at the airport and head toward the administrative offices, and the first thing I'd see were the meeting rooms. It would be no problem. Now, I never felt dumber in my life.

For nearly an hour I walked the area. I was about ready to give up. Our meeting was supposed to start in a couple of minutes. In a last-ditch effort, I went back upstairs to the administrative suite and started rapping on doors and pushing them open, one empty room after another. A typical Latina, I believe in the power of destiny, and I thought maybe it was not meant for me to meet with Senator Reid that day. But, finally, wet with perspiration, almost crying, my feet killing me, I opened a door and there he was — cool, calm, serene, wearing a short-sleeved plaid shirt and khaki pants, sitting at a table across from his elegant wife and a woman who worked in his Reno office. I stood there, my heavy black business suit soaked with perspiration. I was breathless and my nerves were frayed. Taking a seat at the end of the table, I was speechless.

Senator Reid sensed my anxiety. His laid-back demeanor readily put me at ease. "Just relax, and let's talk," he said.

The first thing I did was apologize for being five minutes late. I confessed I had opened the door to every room on the floor until I'd found him.

He accepted my apology.

Then he looked at me in silence for a long moment. The pause grew uncomfortably long. He adjusted his glasses. "Emma, now tell me, why are you running for office?" he finally said. I was touched. People all over the place had been asking me that very same question. But this was the first time I felt someone really cared to learn why I was doing this, what was behind it.

I poured my heart out. I told him that I was born in Argentina, that I had lived in Chile during the coup that brought Pinochet's military dictatorship to power, that I had come to this country and built a good life, and now I wanted to repay the community that had been so wonderful to me. I explained that one of the ways I could show my gratitude was to dedicate myself to political service.

Senator Reid asked me many questions. He wanted to know my campaign platform, and my take on various issues. My interview with him was an educational experience. I learned from his political astuteness and knowledge of the political history of Nevada and the United States. Senator Reid is the sort of politician I dreamed of being. In my opinion, he is truly a servant of the public, not just a professional politician. For me he is a champion of social issues, education and minority issues. He has a strong social conscience. We differed only in our views on abortion. He had never waffled in his position, and for that I deeply respected him. At the same time he had voted consistently for bills relating to other women's issues, such as stopping domestic violence and child abuse and supporting child care.

We covered a lot of ground in our meeting. We talked for a long time about the harsh realities of running for office. He made it clear it was not an easy road. Then he looked at his wife across the table and said, "You know, I really like Emma. What do you think?"

She had listened carefully to everything I'd said. But I was taken aback. They were going to talk about me in my presence? She gave him a large smile and didn't say anything.

The Senator stood. "Well, Emma," he said, shaking my hand, "I will do everything I can to help you win this election." From that day on, Senator Reid was a source of energy and great support for my campaign.

For any political neophyte running for office, one of the most difficult tasks is asking for campaign contributions. For me, it was extremely hard. Asking for money seemed absurd. If I represented what people wanted to see elected, why did I need to go and ask them for money? However, calling people on the phone and asking, "Can you please send a check?" and not only that but asking, "Can you send a $500 check?" is required in today's political campaigns. Even calling some of my closest friends and saying, "As you well know, I'm running for office. Could you send a check?" forced me to swallow my pride. And it never really became any easier.

One thing that helped was the training from the Women's Political Fund in Washington, D.C. This group worked to get women elected to office. It held a training session in Seattle for some 150 candidates from across the nation. One of the many objectives of the seminar was to train women to ask for money. Here, the lesson was brutally frank: If you don't go and get the money, you can't get your message out. And if you don't get your message out, people won't vote for you.

How much money did I need to raise? When they told me $100,000, I thought they were kidding. To throw away $100,000 on a campaign race when some of my constituents earned $4.25 an hour and were practically starving, seemed utterly irrational. Think of how many kids you could send to college, or how you could open a childcare center for Latino children with $100,000. And now I had to spend that amount just to get my message out? Surely there was another way. Couldn't I just go door-to-door?

The trainers drummed into us the concept that you must pay the media to reach your audience. To imprint your message, you must buy advertisement after advertisement after advertisement. The seminar also reinforced the importance of lobbyists. We were repeatedly told, "Call them, meet with them, ask them about their concerns and tell them that you need money and how much money you need."

I discovered during my campaign that lobbyists fall into two groups. The first group are lobbyists hired to disseminate information about the clients they represent. They get to know political candidates and they determine those candidates most concerned with their clients' issues, and therefore who deserve their help to get elected. The second group of lobbyists are those who play both sides of an election. They contribute to a campaign regardless of a candidate's policy stances. What they desire is access, rather than specific policy outcomes.

I went to lunch with some of the lobbyists who said they were impressed with me, who believed I could win and thought I'd make an effective senator. However, they confided that my opponent has been so kind to them and their clients that they just couldn't take the chance of backing me. Some of these lobbyists had been around the block a dozen times. They were both career lobbyists and political consultants. These political consultants could work both sides of the fence. They could work for a candidate and then be hired by a special interest group afterwards to lobby the very candidate they had helped get into office. It seemed unethical to me, but it isn't illegal and it certainly could be lucrative for those who indulged in this practice.

One of the big issues concerning lobbyists was tort reform, and I was caught in the middle. I have a great respect for physicians in this country, and some local doctors and their spouses have been close friends for years. Doctors believe that lawyers and personal injury lawsuits are responsible for the rise in their malpractice insurance costs over the years, even though there is no clear evidence to support that belief. Several years earlier the physicians had helped pass legislation that established a panel to screen lawsuits, ostensibly to eliminate "frivolous" suits. While the lawyers were satisfied with the panel, the doctors were not. The doctors now wanted to put a monetary cap on personal injury awards.

Despite my personal feelings for some of the doctors and their families, I was very uncomfortable about putting a monetary cap on compensation for pain and suffering. The doctors' lobby wanted to limit settlements to $250,000. I could conceive of many situations where the limit would not be enough to compensate pain and suffering or to deter future malpractice. In addition, I had come from a country where doctors are essentially immune from responsibility for any wrongdoing. I do not believe that immunity promotes good medical practice by allowing doctors to escape responsibility for damage they may cause. I spent many hours with the president-elect of the local medical association, Dr. John Gray, discussing the doctors' position on tort reform. The doctors' lobbyist never wanted to meet with me. Despite what I learned from discussing the issue, I felt the doctors had sufficient protection from the screening panel and I did not support tort reform. In spite of that, however, I did receive many checks from doctors.

It was a different story with the teachers' association. I was eager to meet its lobbyist. I knew my opponent had voted against the class-size reduction bill that would have mandated one teacher per 15 elementary school students beginning with the third grade.

"I'm glad to sit down and talk to you because, after all, I have devoted my life to education and would like at least tell you how I feel about certain issues," I told the teachers' association lobbyist.

The man looked at me. "I'm sorry, but we already endorsed your opponent," he said.

"What?" I said. "You guys didn't even interview me! You don't know what I think, how supportive I would be. I would definitely support your bills, because they affect what I believe in."

The man was unmoved. "Welcome to politics," he said.

I counted it a moral victory that, in the steady stream of $10 a $50 checks to arrive in the mail, contributions from teachers were numerous. These contributors felt directly, every working day, the effects of my opponent's voting record. These small checks also reflected the anti-incumbent sentiment.

Then there were the senior citizens who were worried about their futures should the Republicans capture a Senate majority. Some contributors included little notes with their checks saying they knew my opponent personally and disliked him as an insensitive politician who had, in recent years, lost touch with the public.

To raise money I also needed to contact the biggest power-brokers in Nevada, the casinos. I spoke with one of the few remaining hotel-casino sole proprietors left in the state. The owner was a man of Basque heritage, and he was extremely kind to grant me an interview. He patiently listened while I expounded on some of my issues. He said he'd send me some money after the primary, although he never did. At least not directly. Some of his officers did attend some of my fund-raisers and donated money. The Las Vegas casinos were the more generous source of money.

I had no problem accepting money from the casinos. I consider myself pro-gaming but do not believe everything the casinos do is right. The casinos need to provide better wages and protection for workers. Most casinos lack child-care for their employees. Nor do they promote responsible growth: huge high-rise hotel-casinos keep going up, without the concomitant addition of affordable housing. Minimum wage does not cover the rent of adequate housing for families, much less health insurance, food and utilities. Nevertheless, gaming is our state's economic bread-and-butter, and I wanted the casinos to remain a thriving industry.

And so, step by step, I was climbing up the mountain toward raising $100,000.

Of the 150 candidates from every state in the nation, I was the only Latina candidate for public office who had attended the Woman's Political Fund seminar. There were only a few African Americans and no Native Americans in Seattle. If the women's movement was achieving power, that power was best reflected among Anglo women. Even now, there is only small political space for minority women in the American political system. And in the state of Nevada the representation is pitifully worse.

While most of the speakers at the seminar were Anglo women, I was most affected by the speech from a black woman who had won election as a district attorney in Indiana. She related how difficult her campaign had been and how she was forced to fight daily attacks on her ethnicity. During her presentation, I entertained the thought that maybe it was too early for me, too soon for a Latina, to be elected in Nevada.

But I would find out. It was now June 30th: the day of our big kick-off campaign party. The yellow fliers we sent out read: EMMA SEPULVEDA, Senate District 4 — Democrat, "A Voice of Integrity and Commitment for Our Community."

At the party there would be food, music and dancing, "Fun for The Whole Family" at the Musician's Hall. The donation was $10 for adults, $15 for couples, and children admitted free. We mailed out several thousand fliers.

About 500 people showed up. I was proud of the turnout. A group of local musicians played party blues and rock 'n' roll. The hall was decked out in blue and yellow, with big signs, balloons and flowers everywhere. The volunteers had worked very hard, and the food was delicious.

My former boss' restaurant, Miguel's, had donated tacos despite the fact that he had called that morning and told me, "Emma, I need to talk to you. How come you never told me you were a Democrat?"

That night would be the first time I had to stand up and deliver a political address to a large gathering. I avoided a prepared script. Instead, I spoke from my heart. I thanked the people who were making the real sacrifices in the campaign, John and Jonathan. Jonathan wouldn't have Mommy reading stories to him at night. John wouldn't have a wife to spend time as his companion. I briefly elucidated my positions on the issues and explained why I believed I needed to run. I said it was time to restore power to the people, to control the Senate and stop the special interests from running our state. At several points I was interrupted by clapping and chants of "Emma, Emma!" The enthusiasm of my supporters caused a lump to form in my throat. I found it difficult to carry on. Tears came to my eyes and I fought them all the way to the end of my speech.

At the same time the energy of the gathering created a surge of power within me. Such energy elevates, makes you feel invincible, makes you think there are no limits and that anything is possible. I told everyone with complete confidence that I would win. Throughout my short speech, I stole glances at my son Jonathan. He seemed in awe. He clearly winced every time the group called out his mom's name. He was embarrassed that his mom was in front of everybody speaking about him. I think he had suddenly realized *we are in big, big trouble.* This campaign was larger than his six-year-old mind had imagined. Now it was real and it frightened him. And it frightened me, too.

But at that moment, looking at my American-born son, I realized more than ever how much I loved this country and how wonderful it would be to be part of its history as the first Latina woman immigrant to serve in the Nevada Senate. I knew that I was making this sacrifice for all the right reasons, that I was doing it for my son, for all the little brown faces that were in the audience, who one day might follow in my footsteps. Other speakers followed: Yolanda, my Mexican friend; Jan Evans, my assemblywoman friend; and the president of the local AFL-CIO chapter.

The evening went splendidly. The party faithfully had come forth in force. The local television news cameras were on hand to capture it for that night's broadcasts. All told, we raised about $3,000. More importantly, we seemed to have harnessed the enormous energy that is generated when people believe that change can occur that reflects their hopes and dreams.

John, Jonathan and I departed the hall that night with, "Emma, Emma!" still ringing in our ears. In the car my son put his little hands around my face, looked straight into my eyes, and said to me in Spanish, his language for intimate moments, *"mami yo sé que tú vas a ganar y eso me da mucho miedo."* ["Mom, I know you are going to win and that scares me so much."]

We went home entirely convinced that I *was* going to prevail.

Are You A Beaner?

DRIVING AROUND MY DISTRICT, acclimating myself in the aftermath of filing for office, was one thing. Now I had to knock on doors.

Walking up to a strange home and pushing a doorbell or rapping on a door takes a lot of strength. You're invading someone's private space. You're asking to be invited into another person's home. What's more, you never know whom, or what, awaits you behind each portal. You wish for the wisdom held by the streetwise cop, the taxi driver, the pizza deliverer or the door-to-door salesman. The grassroots politician, armed only with that tenuous bromide known as democracy, peddles earnestness and an abstract political platform to an increasingly disaffected and detached citizenry.

No wonder most established politicians and incumbents evade taking their campaigns to doorsteps! I faced knocking on hundreds of doors as a brown-skinned Latina with a foreign accent. And I was selling not only myself but politics, a subject loaded with emotion.

As I geared up for the door-knocking phase of my campaign, I couldn't ignore the disturbing fact that my very appearance would make me unpopular among certain segments of the district. To some, I was the embodiment of the enemy. Not only was I a woman running for office, but I was a dark-eyed foreigner: a real outsider to the community. There were women who still embraced the belief that a woman's place is in the background. There were outspoken legions who march self-righteously under an ill-defined banner of "conservative," bashing an even more amorphous group they brand "liberal."

Meeting these constituents should have filled me with foreboding in the politically polarized year of 1994, when a petty and general hostility toward "government" was pervasive.

If one factor was in my favor, it was that I was a political neophyte. Enthusiasm was my key trait. Thank God for it, too. I discovered on my first evening of canvassing that I was quite unprepared for the sheer physical work. Door-to-door canvassing requires hoofing it, with no breaks, for sometimes four or five hours. You forgo food and water because you know you won't have access to a restroom. Your knees and feet hurt and you suffer the fatigue that comes from being constantly "on" when you make cold contacts. By the time my canvassing campaign ended five months later, I had lost thirty pounds.

Then there were the mental stressors. I didn't consider that many households have dogs, and some homes have as many as five! And we're not talking toy poodles. Envision a ferocious-looking Rottweiler or German Shepherd bounding around a corner as you open a front gate. Unlike a mail carrier, I carried no protective spray. Sometimes I'd already be on the porch when a person would open the screen door and a dog larger than I suddenly jumped on me before the owner could control it.

I will never forget the day when one of those dogs jumped so quickly I fell flat on my back. The young Saint Bernard was licking my face and neck. I was on the grass, under an uncontrolled beast twice my size, when the owner came out and said, "If Buff loves you so much, that means you are a good person, so you have my vote."

I sincerely appreciated her support, but at the time I would have liked it more if she had taken that enormous animal off of me. And so my "dog days of summer" became a challenge of endurance and perseverance.

Going door-to-door was essential to my campaign. My consultant, David, was surprised at my ambition to walk the precincts because he was used to running big campaigns in districts of 100,000 or 200,000 registered voters, where such canvassing would have been impractical. Many such consultants believed that contacting only a small percentage of households made no significant difference at the polls. My Republican opponent had walked his district as a Democrat, but had given up the practice later. Some of the district's older residents told me they remembered his showing up on their doorsteps, years earlier. These constituents appreciated the chance to meet a candidate face-to-face instead of being bombarded by 30-second sound bites on TV or radio.

The canvassing proved enlightening for me. It confirmed that my issues were important to voters, and it also informed me about other issues I hadn't previously considered important. In retrospect, I found canvassing held some of the best and worst moments of the campaign. Going door-to-door is the only way to find out whether you are speaking the same language as the voters (in my case with a slight accent, too!). I certainly learned far more from this grassroots work than from all the literature I read and all my attendance at candidate nights and breakfasts and information panels. It amazed me that so many residents remembered candidates who had canvassed their neighborhoods in years past. According to them, those candidates had tried to "connect" with their constituents. Such a sentiment among voters was for me a revelation.

My door-to-door plan called for marathon canvassing. I would go out Saturday through Thursday from early June up to and including the September primary election, hitting as many homes of the 29,000 registered voters as possible. Little by little, I tailored my walking campaign. Usually I would start at 4 p.m. and conclude around 9 p.m., as darkness fell. John was my first door-to-door partner. We took Jonathan along for the first week, so the public would be introduced to my family. But Jonathan hated the experience. He was only six years old and walking tired him out. He grew easily distracted, playing with people's dogs or sprinklers, and proved to be more of a liability than an asset. He took every chance he could to make faces at people while I was trying to convince them to vote for me.

John also proved somewhat of a hindrance. As my husband, he felt very protective. When voters didn't react positively toward me, it hurt him. He had a hard time digesting it. He took it as a personal attack. At first, the rejection hurt me, too. "My God," I'd think, "how many times can I be rejected in one day?" But I soon became hardened. I'd shrug off a negative encounter and continue on to the next address.

My steady door-to-door traveling partners became Cristina, Jim, who was one of my former university students and who had become an optometrist, and my good friend Pam. On weekends, a dozen volunteers might fan out into the streets of a designated area such as Hidden Valley, where the houses are widely separated. More rural areas offered such obstacles as snakes and rats. The Holcomb Lane neighborhood at the southernmost edge of the district has ranches where the front porches could be a mile walk from the road. I'd hike up an unpaved road only to be greeted by a hostile, territorial canine whose bark scared the daylights out of me, and whose master wasn't home. Then, inevitably in such situations, my eyes would fall upon a sign warning that absolutely no solicitors were welcome. And so I'd beat a long retreat in defeat. Such was the gritty reality of running for office.

Canvassing also turned out to be a complicated business. Even deciding how to dress had required much thought at the outset. Some in the committee said I looked too young to be taken seriously, with my long straight hair. They counseled me to wear outfits that made me look more serious and mature. But more importantly, I needed to look more "American."

The conventional wisdom about canvassing is that you visit only those residences with registered Democrats. From the beginning, I bucked the advice of my committee and decided also to go to homes where residents weren't registered. I'd bring them information to encourage voter registration. My goal was to register every Latino in my district, so that the Latino community could have a continuing impact. Sometimes this registration effort would be fruitful. Quite often, however, the resistance of some citizens turned into hostility.

"I don't see one reason why I should go vote," I'd be told.

"Things are worse than they have ever been, and I feel like voting is just giving them [politicians] more encouragement."

The Latinos would ask, "Why should I vote? Nobody listens to us, nobody cares about our lives."

That was the political atmosphere I encountered. Then there were the many who had recently moved to town and didn't consider voting a priority. In the end, I realized that many people I had met face-to-face would never vote for me or any other candidate.

The cynicism ran deep. There was an aimless anger at "the government." On more than one occasion a person looked at me with pity and said something like, "Why would a nice lady like you want to get into politics? It's the dirtiest, most disgusting business there is." "What," they asked, "could possibly be your reason?"

At the end of a four- or five-hour door-knocking excursion, we'd load the pickup truck full of campaign signs and return to the households that had given us permission to post signs. It was hard work, but it had to be done. It also provided reinforcement for the daily work. As I drove back through the area the next day and saw all the signs we had placed, it gave me a sense of accomplishment. Here were the hard-won, tangible results of going door-to-door. Here were the advertisements that would give me the sorely needed name recognition. On the downside, sometimes I would pass through an area a day or two later and the signs would be gone. It was dirty pool but another harsh reality of campaigning. My only consolation was that those households that had had signs stolen recognized that my opponents were playing dirty politics.

The entire committee became convinced that face-to-face contact was imperative. I had also to counter the negative effects of the strong support for Proposition 187 in California as well as anti-immigrant feelings throughout the state. So into the trenches I went.

I had some very touching encounters. The first was with

George, a gentleman in his eighties and a lifelong Democrat who lived in a corner brick house on Nixon Street. I knocked on his door one day. I was ready to pass out from the heat. I had drained my water bottle of melted ice I carried with me.

"Honey!" he exclaimed. "You look exhausted. I bet you haven't had dinner. You are soaked. You are tired. Are you okay? Come into my house."

I had been told never to walk into anybody's home. But I broke this rule a number of times in my canvassing period, especially with older people. George looked like a grandfather waiting to rescue me. I waved to Cristina and went inside. I sat in his living room. George went to his refrigerator and brought over an ice cream bar and a glass of juice.

He sat down. "Are you sure you want to go into this [politics]?" he said. "It's a tough world."

George, it turned out, knew everything about me. He had read every newspaper article about me, and he knew everything about my opponent. He even had clipped out candidate surveys from the newspaper. He was up to speed on everyone running for office in his district. George also knew the lay of the local political land. He told me how rough it was to go up against the old boys in Reno.

"You are running against the establishment," he said. "I used to work in the casino industry. This is a tough world, especially for somebody like you."

He wasn't telling me anything I didn't know. But he was certainly confirming it. Then he surprised me.

After pointing out the impossibility of my winning, he said, "I want one of your signs in my yard. You'll have all my support, and I'm going to talk to as many people as I can so you will be elected. One of my dreams before I die is to see people like you get in office."

Here was a man who personified the democratic tradition. I had made a friend. Even after I'd finished canvassing his precinct, I'd return from time to time to visit George. Sometimes he'd call my campaign headquarters and say, "Tell Emma if she's driving by here to stop, because I have these enormous, juicy tomatoes from my garden." He was my democratic guardian angel.

I had a moving experience of a different kind with a woman in her forties who lived in a duplex off Moran Street, in Central Reno. It was a Saturday afternoon, about one o'clock. She had evidently just awakened to answer my knock. Her makeup was smeared. Her hair was ratty. She stood there in her robe looking at me as I talked. I could smell alcohol on her breath. She looked emaciated, anorexic, and her eyes were puffy.

"Tell me about yourself, how you came to this country, what you are doing," she said. She wanted to know about my life more than my platform positions. Then she started crying. "You know what?" she said. "I wish I had the courage to fight in this life like you are. I work in a casino the whole day, then I get off work and I start drinking. Then I come home and I drink some more until I get drunk. Then I sleep most of the day and I get up and go to work, and I work so I can get drunk again."

She was sobbing. "I would give anything, anything, to be in your place," the woman said. "And this is my country. I didn't take the opportunity to enjoy what this country has to give to somebody like you. Look at the difference between you and me today."

I was so sad, I began to cry, too.

"I don't know what went wrong," she said, "but people in this country don't enjoy the most wonderful things that we have, this land of opportunity, this land of the free.

"You know," she said, "I'm not feeling very good these days. But I can promise you that for election day, I'll be there casting my vote for you."

I gave her a bumper sticker. She asked me for two. She wanted to put one in her bedroom so she would remember me. I still think about driving by her house sometimes and spending a few minutes talking with her again.

There were also those moments when I couldn't help but smile. Several older women told me I was "too young" to run for the senate. "What are you doing, little girl, running for the U.S. Senate? What is your experience?" they'd ask.

"Oh, I'm running for the *state* Senate," I'd say.

"Well, don't you have children?" they'd say. "Who is going to take care of your kids? Shouldn't you be home cooking and taking care of your kids instead of wasting your time going door-to-door, trying to be in politics? This is a man's world, honey."

Some would stand in the doorway and say, "Oh, you are so cute! You are much prettier in person than in your picture. I have seen your billboard, and I thought, 'Oh, what a pretty lady,' but now I see you are so much prettier! I really like your smile." The first few times I ran into this attitude, I felt like snapping back: "Don't you have anything more important to say?" But I soon reached the conclusion that it was good to know that some people took the time to make positive comments. I decided to take the compliments. In fact, as time went on and I became more experienced at my job, I found that I could use their flattery to my advantage.

"Oh, how *sweet* of you!" I'd respond, breaking into a sunny smile. "Could I have your support on November eighth?" I'd ask in a sugary voice. Who knew? Maybe I won over the votes of those kind older women who characterized me as "that cute little Emma with a darling accent."

I stood in front of a house on Mustang Circle. A sports utility vehicle sat in the driveway. Sprinklers danced jets of water in a pattern that overshot the lawn and dampened my clothes as I raced up the walkway to the door. I hoped that a growling dog wouldn't suddenly materialize and intercept me. Cristina waited back on the sidewalk. We had learned that if both of us approached a house, the occupant assumed we were evangelists and did not answer our knock or opened the door only to slam it shut with a curt, "We're Catholic," or, "We're Mormon."

As I prepared to knock at this Mustang Circle house, I psyched myself up. Already it had been a long day, but I told myself, "You have to do it. You have to do it. The only way you can win is by going door-to-door. There could be five votes

in this house. This is how you can win." Standing on the doorstep, I thought about how to strike the balance between being
too lively and too grave. I wanted to come across as compassionate yet firm in my ideas and well-versed on the issues. I rang the
doorbell and waited. There was no response, but I sensed someone was home. My information card noted that the residence
contained registered Democrats. I wanted to contact them.

During my training, I had been advised not to ring a door
bell twice. Often, however, I ignored this advice. I pushed the
button again and heard the chimes reverberating inside. The door
was opened by a boy about ten years old. I asked, "Can I speak
with your parents, please?"

He called, "Mom!" In a few moments, a neatly dressed
woman approached and looked at me quizzically.

I smiled. "Good evening," I began. "My name is Emma
Sepúlveda and I'm running for the state senate in District 4. I'm
here to ask you if I can have your support. I would like to talk
about any concerns or issues that you might have."

"Well, what are you going to do about providing safe streets?"
she asked.

"I believe we need to look at the reasons for the increase in
crime," I said. "I want to put more money into preventing crimes
before they become crimes, instead of building more prisons."
This view was not a popular one. People kept saying the same
thing over and over: they wanted people locked up; they wanted
more prisons. And "truth in sentencing" was a big issue.

The nicely dressed woman looked at me and in front of her
son she screamed, "Put them behind bars, or even better, shoot
them! It is just like the people in my church said, women should
never be in office because they are soft on crime!"

Her attitude was not unusual. Surveys showed people were
not as concerned about tax increases to fund more prisons as
they were about assuring that sentences meted out were fully
served by the convicted. And if a killer is sentenced to death,
they wanted the government to carry out the execution quickly.
Almost everywhere, I encountered the same response: people

wanted more prisons, longer prison terms and an end to early parole. Older people were saying, "I don't want my money to go for education, I want more money to go for prisons."

They wanted more police in the streets, ironically echoing what President Clinton wanted in his crime bill, yet at the same time they attacked the president. And they wanted capital punishment for sex offenders and child abusers. They resented "baby sitting" convicted murderers with color TVs and exercise rooms.

People felt unsafe in their own homes. And they were right to feel that way. In fact, I was shocked to see doors pocked with bullet holes in some areas such as Neil Road and Central Reno. One building was so riddled with bullet holes that the sight of it filled me with fear, as if someone were ready at any moment to open fire and blow my head off.

One time I was canvassing on a street off Wells Avenue. No one would answer my knocking. Finally, a door at a brick duplex opened. It was a Latina woman. She quickly grabbed me and tugged me inside.

"*M'hija* (my daughter), don't you know they just had a drive-by shooting here? The police are cruising around. Didn't you see their cars? They're following people."

Everything I'd heard about crime in the city — which I had planned to work on if elected — was no longer an abstract concept. It was brutal reality. People were getting shot. People were dying in the heart of my district and I did not think that the incumbent state senator cared. These experiences also confirmed my belief that politicians were more interested in pandering to the public's cry for more prisons than in finding the reasons why children turned to criminal behavior or in providing programs to eradicate those causes.

My opponent's TV commercials showed him dressed in a three-piece suit with suspenders in a setting at a make-believe crime scene. He ducked under the yellow tape and told the public that we needed to put criminals behind bars and keep them there.

How different we were. I was walking door-to-door in a

section of my district where shootings occurred all too frequently and my opponent was postering on a phony TV set in an attempt to get people to believe he knew something about crime in our lives and had a plan to stop it. I often wondered where he had been with this plan during the past twelve years that he had been in office.

I learned early on in my canvassing to look for the little "NRA" stickers on screen doors. Some gun owners are proud of their membership in the National Rifle Association, and from the moment I introduced myself they wanted to know where I stood on the 1994 Crime Bill and its provision to ban some assault weapons. President Clinton wanted to limit the sale of "assault weapons." Gun enthusiasts contended that the category of "assault weapon" had been an arbitrary and inappropriate designation, since the possession of firearms, for whatever purpose, was a right guaranteed by the Constitution. The National Rifle Association maintained the position that all firearms, including assault weapons, should remain available.

I had read the crime bill from beginning to end. From my own experience, I believed that the only use for an assault weapon was to be able to kill as many people or animals as possible, as quickly as possible. I was raised in a family of hunters; my grandfathers, father and brother all were hunters. I believe we have the right to bear arms and keep rifles in our houses. But I do not believe that we are entitled to carry grenades in our car, or buy military-style weapons with which we could terrorize the community. Similarly, I believed in the requirement for background checks and a waiting period for people purchasing firearms, so somebody with a history of criminal activity or mental illness couldn't go into a gun store and buy a weapon. I also don't believe minors should be allowed to own guns.

Many crime bill opponents in District 4 were very angry with U.S. Senator Harry Reid because he was a strong supporter of the bill. Under my photograph on my campaign brochure it read, "Sen. Harry Reid, Honorary Campaign Chair."

Sometimes, an NRA member would glance at my brochure,

spot the reference to Senator Reid and become furious. "Oh, so you're just like Senator Reid, and you're going to come here and confiscate our guns and give them to the criminals and spend our tax dollars on midnight basketball and you think that's going to get rid of the gangs."

At the beginning of July, I approached the door of an attached home. Before I could even ring the bell, a man in his thirties, short-haired and very muscular like a body builder, swung the door open and barked, "What do you want?!"

I introduced myself.

"Good, good, that's what I've wanted," he said. "I want to talk to one of those goddamned people running for office. What do you think about this stupid crime bill?"

I looked at him. I was going to start speaking when he interrupted again.

"Wait a minute," he said. "Before you tell me what you think, I want to show you this."

It was one of those homes where you open the front door and it leads right into a little living room. I looked where he was pointing. Leaning against the fireplace was a huge shotgun.

"Do you see this?" he said.

"Oh yeah, I do," I said.

"What do you think about that?!" the man said.

"Well, you have the right to have that," I said. Then, trying to calm him down, I added, "I would put it out of the reach of children."

His TV was on. I believe the evening news had just come on. I guessed that a report on the crime bill had just been broadcast, and that was what had riled him up.

"Well, now, tell me, what do you think about this goddamned stupid thing!" he said.

I said, "What can I tell you? I support it. I do think that we need to have some control over certain arms."

I began to rattle off my view that our Founding Fathers hadn't intended every citizen to have the right to bear any type of device designed to kill people. . . ."

"Shut up fucking bitch!" the man said.

It was the end of our discussion. He was in full tirade mode. Maybe he was having a steroid rage.

"That's enough," he said. "I'm telling you, and all the supporters, I'll be the first one to shoot any sonofabitch who walks in my driveway, or just gets close to my family, my car, my house, anything. And no one, not even your fucking president, is going to come to my house and take this gun from me. I'll shoot *everybody*. And you know what? I'm going to get more guns like this, because now I know that you guys are going to arm the criminals. You are giving the choice to the criminals to go arm themselves, because they're going to buy these assault weapons anyway on the black market. So *I'm* going to be the one that's going to be unprotected. So now, if you don't turn around and get your fucking ass off my property, I'm going to go get my gun and blow your brains out."

He turned around and started walking toward his shotgun.

I remember running so fast down his sloping driveway and thinking, "This guy's probably going to shoot me! I'm dead, right here." With every step I took on the rest of that block, I trained a nervous eye on that man's door to see if it was open.

During the rest of the walk, I remembered that I had survived the military coup in Chile nineteen years ago and I realized that now I could be shot in a second by a fanatic only because I told him that I support the Crime Bill and that I like President Clinton. Life can be full of dramatic ironies.

Parents, especially working parents, repeatedly expressed concern about the availability of after-school programs for children. The parents worked until 5 p.m.; the children came home from school at 3 p.m. What latchkey programs there were weren't available to everyone and, in any case, they cost money. My belief that all communities drastically need affordable child-care was depressingly reaffirmed by the number of unattended children I witnessed on my door-to-door rounds. Everywhere in the district were children taking care of children. A ten-year-old would open the door to an apartment, cradling a baby. There were sometimes five children running around an apartment, unsupervised.

Then there were the parents who were often under the influence of drugs or alcohol. A parent would open the door, inebriated, reeking, perhaps popping open a beer can, while babies in dirty diapers played in the background. Sometimes, the house would be very unkempt; you could smell and see pet feces on the floor. The first thing the adult would do was turn around and shout angrily at the children to shut up or to get away from the door. Then he or she would ask me what I wanted.

Almost as tragic were the pregnant mothers answering doors of one-room apartments. Behind them would be three or four other children running around. These "poor" were so numerous, the poverty so pervasive, it almost seemed that a vast section of Reno was part of the Third World.

Should I have been surprised? The sad reality is that a great percentage of our county's labor pool is composed of minimum-wage, service industry workers. They are trapped in low-paying jobs and their children are the most vulnerable victims. A parent cannot feed one or more children, go to work full time, and afford child-care on $4.25 an hour. To do so successfully would be the miracle of miracles.

When I had the opportunity, I spoke to business leaders about a commitment from them to help create private-public funds for more child-care facilities. One model child-care arrangement was located at the area's largest hospital, Washoe Medical Center, and another was the child-care system at International Game Technology, a Reno-based manufacturer of slot machines. It could be done in Reno.

One of my central platform positions was that it had to be done.

In addition to crime and child-care, health-care issues were a high priority for the constituents in my district. "Social medicine" was a catch phrase I kept hearing repeated. I had trouble with this concept, having lived in two nations in South America with some type of socialized medicine. The Chilean and Argentinean systems suffered from inadequate resources and therefore weren't models we should follow. On the other hand, these residents were correct in assuming that something needed to be done in Nevada. Nevada has some of the most expensive health-care costs in the nation. At the same time, it ranks near the top of the list in the number of people who have no health insurance.

The conditions I confronted when working with senior citizens depicted a similarly pressing social need. Walking in the lower middle-class areas in Central Reno and elsewhere, I met numerous retirees who didn't have enough money to enter a good retirement home, yet had too much money to be taken care of by their government. So they lived by themselves, totally unattended. Just like the children of single mothers, they were practically abandoned. The abandoned were desperately lonely to talk to somebody who would listen. Often, I'd oblige them with a lengthy visit, for which I would be taken to task by my walking companion and my committee: "Don't spend too much time talking to people," they'd say. But sometimes, I just couldn't help myself. My heart ached. I'd sit in their living rooms trying not to be overwhelmed by their stories or cry in front of them.

Many were not only starved for attention but also under great physical and emotional strain. A man on Tonopah Street told me that he had fallen down, broken his hip and been unable to reach a phone to call 911 because of his unbearable pain. He'd spent the night on the kitchen floor. At four or five in the morning he finally inched his way with wrenching effort to his phone and made the call for help.

Some seniors told me they were constantly faced with this choice: Do I buy groceries or my prescription medicine? Do I stay sick and in pain or get a meal? Social Security only goes so far. And these seniors were anything but freeloaders. Often I would drive home thinking that these were the people who had built America. We have a high quality of life today in this country because of their hard work. Here they were in their "golden years" and they had been all but abandoned. What had become of their families? Their spouses had died, their children were grown and living in other cities.

They were on fixed incomes although prices and taxes kept going up. The Nevada senior aid programs were insufficient. I knew we needed a state program to provide more discount allowances for seniors to buy medication. We needed more transportation programs for seniors who are trapped at home because they cannot get insurance, are unable to drive, or because of temporary health problems. Outreach efforts to let seniors know about these services were also necessary.

Some people I spoke with nurtured dreams of publicly funded, universal health care. I believed that what was now possible was universal access, not fully funded, public medical care. I was concerned that if the health-care system was funded by the public, there would never be adequate funding set aside and there would be two separate systems that afforded very unequal levels of care for the rich and the poor. Poor people would end up dying while waiting to see a doctor. In Chile, a poor working person could wait months for surgery, but a wealthy person with connections could go to an expensive clinic and have surgery in a matter of hours.

If people pay what they can afford with their employers covering the remaining cost, then both employers and their workers receiving the care have an interest in assuring good health care and keeping the costs down. We also need to focus more resources on prevention of disease rather than putting so much energy into care after the disease is present. For too long in this country we have forced people to use emergency rooms, one of the most expensive forms of providing health care, to treat health problems that never would have become serious had people had access to basic, inexpensive treatment beforehand.

While I concentrated on the four issues of crime, education, child care and health care, I learned that people were concerned about other issues as well. I had vowed to never lie or equivocate as I went door-to-door. I'd represent myself honestly and forthrightly, no matter how nasty people became. And some did get nasty.

On the issue of school prayer, I was adamant. I supported the use of public school facilities for voluntary religious activities. I am not opposed to a minute of silence in public classrooms for reflection, but there should not be a mandatory prayer that all students are forced to say. For twelve years of my schooling I had been forced to pray daily. I was required to go to Mass every Friday and receive communion. I never had a chance to say, "What if I don't want to?" Americans have religious freedom, and that's one more great thing about this country. For me, this freedom means both freedom from religion as well as freedom to practice one's own religion.

The death penalty? I was for it. As much as I abhorred the political purges and mass killings during the Pinochet regime's reign of terror, I wanted my gay friend's killer, and other criminals like him, to pay in full for the crimes they committed.

Gay rights? I believe that every adult should be free to make whatever consenting choices they want, according to their sexuality, and neither government nor religion should interfere with that highly personal and completely private decision.

Abortion was an issue that invited some of the most heated rhetoric, especially from those people who classify themselves as belonging to the Religious Right. I withstood a great deal of hostility from them, but I accepted their right to verbally express their opinions. My feelings on abortion can never be separated from those haunting memories of parsley and screams I carry with me from my high school days. Interestingly, my opponent also was pro-choice. I pointed out this similarity to the anti-abortionists and sometimes their attitudes toward me would change, and they'd listen to my other views more closely.

Canvassing also taught me that many people voted on the

basis of a desire for change rather than on the basis of specific policy positions.

There were those who would cut me off mid-sentence and say, "Hey, don't worry. I will only vote for a woman in this election!"

There were also men who'd say, "Well, I'm tired of professional male politicians. I think women could make a difference, so you have my vote."

There were even a few self-proclaimed Republicans who would say, "Actually, I'm for term limits and I won't mind voting for a Democrat for a change. You seem to be a different type of candidate, not the average professional politician." So, from this throw-the-bastards-out clique, I captured some votes.

Proposition 187 in California was one more burning issue in 1994 that affected Nevadans as well. While the proposition was solely a California matter, for the moment, the passions it stirred spilled across the border into Nevada. California governor Pete Wilson was the main proponent of this proposition, which was designed, in part, to deny public benefits to what he called, "illegal aliens," but whom I prefer to call, "undocumented workers."

Again, in the heated debate surrounding Proposition 187, it was not an easy time to be a Latina running for office, soliciting votes on doorsteps. At the heart of the popularity of Prop 187 was a deeply embedded dread that Americans were losing their country and culture to "foreigners" who were taking their jobs or, worse, not even working at all but sneaking across the border to have babies who would live off the U.S. government.

Of course, the "foreigners" were mostly Latinos and their families who came north and took whatever jobs they could find. Employers benefit from the influx of undocumented workers because the employer can pay substandard wages and does not have to provide any benefits. Despite this benefit to some small businesses, the idea that these "foreigners" might want to stay north of the border, where life, harsh as it was, wasn't nearly as harsh as in the deprived economic conditions back home, was abominable to Prop 187 supporters.

"What do you think about 187?" and, "Would you support 187 in Nevada?" were frequent questions tossed at me. Like abortion and the crime bill, it was an issue that put me in quick confrontation with many voters. I was certainly against Proposition 187. I tried to explain to people: "You keep giving them jobs, they will keep coming."

"I will never vote for you because you will open the borders," I was told.

There was a couple that lives in a very nice, large home in the Old Southwest in Marsh Street.

"Do you know what Proposition 187 is?" they asked me.

I said I didn't think that legislation was the answer to the problem in California or anywhere else in the United States. So if such a proposition were introduced in Nevada, I would oppose it.

They did not like my answer. "Well, do you mean to tell us I'm paying my taxes so the kids of illegal aliens can go to school here and get free dental care?" they queried. They followed with their list of allegations about the undocumented workers. These "wetbacks" were abusing the welfare system, their children were the ones becoming gang members. The couple grew more and more upset as they spoke.

"If you don't support 187, we'll never support someone like you because you're going to back the agenda of the 'dirty greasers' who are coming here to take our jobs from us."

The wife was especially adamant. "We know all about this, because we used to have a nanny from Guatemala."

I looked at her. "Well, you know why you have a career, because you had that nanny from Guatemala to care for your children," I said. What the hell. I wasn't going to get their vote anyway. They made it clear they would never vote for a "greaser."

I heard many unpleasant words used to describe Latinos in the course of my canvassing. It was all part of the strange patchwork of experiences I accumulated. And some of these strange experiences did not have anything to do with being Latina. Like the one when I was walking in a working-class area near Mill Street, east of the downtown casino core.

At one house, the front door was open but the screen door was closed. I tapped on it. Inside, I could make out a young man lying on a couch, watching TV.

"Yes, m'am?" he said.

"I'm Emma Sepúlveda and I'm running for the state senate in District 4," I said.

It was annoying that, in the summer, people kept their front doors open but wouldn't get up to answer their screen doors because they were busy watching TV or eating dinner and didn't want to be bothered. I'd be stuck standing there on the doorstep where, because of the lighting, they could see me but I couldn't really see them. I tried my best to talk to them through the screen door.

This guy wouldn't even get up off his couch. "So," he shouted through the screen door. "Tell me more. Tell me more about yourself."

I told him briefly what my main issues were. I could sense I was getting nowhere. "Anything else?" I said. I started to leave.

"Oh, just a minute, just a minute!" he said. He got up and walked to the door and opened it. I saw immediately that wasn't all he had opened. He was wearing shorts. His zipper was down. And, yes, he was hanging out.

I looked him straight in the eyes. There was nowhere else I felt I could look.

"Are you any good?" he said.

I had no clue how to respond to such an ambiguous question. Maybe I should have said, "Dirty kid, turn around, your zipper is down!"

He was fairly tall. I was frozen and could look only at his eyes, wondering if he was going to grab my arm and pull me into his living room. The seconds seemed like an eternity. I finally got up the guts to speak. It turned out to be one of those classic lines you utter in a perilous moment.

"I hope I can have your support," I said. Then I turned around and walked away.

The young man closed the screen door as if nothing had happened.

There was one segment of the district where I never had to feel self-conscious about my race. This was, of course, in the predominantly Latino areas. The main response I got from the Hispanic community was an expression of pride to see a candidate who, in the first place, could speak their language, and secondly, who had also come from where they had come in pursuit of the American Dream. They thought that my willingness to tackle politics in their adopted land reflected positively on them.

What unsettled me was the fear these people lived with. Many, at first, thought I was from the Immigration Services: *la migra*. When I knocked on a door, a little child's face would peek through a curtain and say, *"Mamá! Hay una mujer afuera!"* ["Mom, there's a lady outside."]

Then another face, that of the mother, would poke out from behind the curtain. *"Ay mi'hijo! Raul. Hay una mujer afuera. Ve que quiere."* ["See what she wants."]

A third face, that of a man, would appear. He'd look me up and down. The dynamic would always be the same. The man would open the door, often leaving the chain locked, and the kid would serve as the translator.

"Hi, what do you want?" the child would ask.

I would respond in Spanish. *"Yo hablo español. Soy candidata al senado."* ["I speak Spanish. I am a candidate for the senate."]

They were so afraid that they wouldn't realize I was speaking Spanish to them. Unfailingly, the kid would turn around and "translate" for his or her parents, *"Dice que es candidata al senado."* ["She says that she is a candidate for the Senate."]

Then the mom and dad would say, *"Pregúntale que quiere."* ["Ask her what she wants."] And the kid would ask, *"Que quiere?"* ["What do you want?"]

All this in Spanish! The parents still wouldn't have made

the connection that I was a Latina who was canvassing for votes. I'd say to the child in Spanish, "Tell your parents that I want to meet them because I'm a candidate for the Senate and I really need to talk to them." Finally, the chain would come off and the door would open a little bit more.

After this somewhat confusing interaction, my intention would be clear to them. Their mood would change 180 degrees and the hospitality would gush out.

"Venga!" they'd say. ["Come in!"] *"Quiere una cerveza?"* ["Do you want a beer?"]

Sometimes the woman would say, "I'm just making tamalitos. Would you stay and have a tamalito?"

One woman gave me juice. It was the bottled drink from Mexico that is so full of sugar that it made me more thirsty. I drank it down and to be the gracious guest said, "Oooh, this is so nice!" She went back into her kitchen and returned with two more bottles to drink with me.

These people were so giving, so warm, so proud. The scenes could be quite emotional for me. Some parents wanted their children to pose next to me for a photograph. They would call their children over to shake my hand. "This is a candidate," they would say. It was remarkable to them that a candidate would come to their door and speak their language.

I'd have to explain I wasn't a senator, *una senadora*, but a candidate. It made no difference. Their satisfaction was immense. And their children all wanted a bumper sticker for their bicycles and the parents for their cars. One woman handed me a little good luck charm, a *medallita* with a picture of a saint, *la virgin de Guadalupe*, the patron saint of Mexico. The thoughtful woman tied a little pink ribbon on the medallion, kissed it and placed it in my hand. "You know, *m'hija*, tie this in your brassiere where no one can see it, only you, because this is going to help you win the election," she told me earnestly. "If anyone is going to do evil to you this is going to protect you."

The high I would get from these visits would always be accompanied by a low, the realization that very few of my fellow

Latinos were registered to vote. Many weren't citizens, and a large portion were undocumented. They stood little chance of fighting their way forward, as I had done, to achieve the American Dream.

As for those who were citizens, I found it depressing to try to talk to them and make them understand that they needed to vote. "Why should I vote if nobody will listen to me?" they'd say.

The other ones would say, "I can't vote because I don't understand politics in this country."

I'd spend many hours informing them. "Do you know about Proposition 187?" I'd ask. "This type of legislation may come to Nevada one day, and our rights and our children's rights are going to be affected if we don't vote." I'd touch that chord and see what they had to say.

I was impressed by the large number of immigrants who dreamed of returning to their native countries. "I'm not going to register to vote here because I really want to go back. I want to save money and I want to go back to Guatemala," or, "I want to go back to El Salvador when we don't have any more *guerrilla*," or, "I want to go back to Nicaragua when things are better," or, "I want to go back to Mexico, buy some land and spend the last years of my life in my homeland."

The vast majority of these immigrants were Mexican and proud of their heritage. Their houses were spotless. They were poor people with a deep sense of honor and responsibility. All were employed. None of them were having more kids to get bigger welfare checks.

Very few were even aware that public benefits were available. The ones who were undocumented said they didn't even file their taxes because they were "afraid they're gonna get us." They were hesitant to go to an emergency room for treatment for fear they could wind up deported. Almost none of them had health insurance. Although most were Catholics, I received no reproach over my stance on abortion. They were delighted that they could talk about politics with somebody in Spanish.

Their issues were low-paying jobs, education for their children, how to increase their involvement in that education, and how to keep their kids away from drugs and gangs. They wanted the best for their children. They had come in search of a better future for their sons and daughters.

In all, I had not one single negative experience going door-to-door in the Latino community, but I also knew I wouldn't get many votes. Latinos constituted about fourteen percent of District 4's population. Only one-fifth of these Latinos vote. I hoped they would go to the polls and vote, and I hoped they would vote for me.

In upscale Hidden Valley, early on in my canvassing, I walked up to a beautiful home with lavish landscaping. It was a bright Saturday morning. I approached, looking my best, with a big warm smile.

A middle-aged man answered the door. He was wearing shorts and a polo shirt. I assumed he was a retired executive. I launched into my spiel. He stood there listening, not saying a word, scrutinizing my brochure.

I said, "I'd like to talk about issues with you if you have a minute."

He looked up from the brochure.

"Are you a beaner?" he said.

I had never heard that word before. I didn't know what it meant. But then, people often asked me questions unrelated to politics, such as, "What kind of perfume do you have on?" So I took his question in stride. When you show up on someone's doorstep, they ask what they want. You're in their space; you're at their disposal. You just have to take it and smile. Especially if you're running for office.

"Excuse me?" I said. "I don't know what that means."

He started laughing. "You mean you don't know what a beaner is? Y'know, you are one. It's like a wetback."

Then I got it. I'd been called "wetback" so many times in the United States. Yes, I really did get his meaning.

"I'm not a wetback. I don't even know how to swim," I said. "But I do like beans a lot. I think they are very good for you, full of protein."

He did not appreciate my joke.

"Well," he said, "you know what? I have never supported a beaner. And I will never support one in my life. So you are wasting your time."

He shut the door in my face.

I was far from crushed. Actually, I could not stop laughing. It was pretty funny to be called a "beaner." I was amazed I had never heard the term before. But as sometimes happens when you learn a new word, it seems like you start running into it over and over, as if it had just been invented.

The next time in the campaign I heard it was when someone was talking about my friend, Yolanda, who, as I previously noted, had become the first Latina to head the state taxation department. I was attending a Democratic fund-raising event. I overheard a man telling a group, "Our Governor was looking for a bean-counter, and he literally found one to head the tax department."

This double entendre drew hearty laughter. And people say Americans have no sense of humor.

Another interesting experience came when I was canvassing off Mira Loma Drive in southeast Reno. I found myself in an area where the streets bore Christian names, including Gracia de Dios (Grace of God). It was a middle-class neighborhood. I stopped at a nice house. A middle-aged man with a book in his hand opened the door. His reading glasses were halfway down his nose and he looked intelligent and friendly.

I gave him my spiel.

"Oh," he said. "Where are you from?"

I was always careful how I answered this question. "Actually I'm an American citizen," I said, "but I was born in Argentina and raised in Chile."

"Well, what do you think about abortion?" he said.

"Oh great," I thought. You always have a 50-50 chance of being able to continue your conversation after being asked this question. So I told him how I felt about abortion. That is, I believe every woman should know that abortion is one of the most horrible things she might have to go through in her life. It's not glamorous; it's a horrible experience. But, at the same time, no one should be able to force a woman to have a baby she doesn't want.

The man said, "You know, you just really piss me off. Because you guys breed like rabbits, and you are the worst criminals. Because then you go and have abortions, and you want the government to pay for them, and you use abortion as a contraceptive. And you all are going to rot in hell. You and all your wetback Spaniard criminals who believe in abortion."

I maintained my poise.

"Well, that is your opinion," I said, "and I will respect your opinion. I would never force you to have an abortion, so I don't think you have the right to force me to have a baby."

"Just get out of here," he said, pushing my shoulder so violently that I almost fell on my back.

I closed my eyes in fear of falling. When I opened them again the door was closed.

Then there was the gentleman I encountered at a nice home on Lakeside Drive, about a mile north of my home. I still drive by this house on my way home. It has become a landmark for me.

It was another Saturday morning. The man was about sixty. He opened the door and I ran through my short speech.

"You know what?" he said. "All you goddamn Mexicans should go back where you came from. How could you dare come and live in our country and take our country away and just come and kill us? Let me tell you," he said.

"See that lake?" He pointed at nearby Virginia Lake, a little man-made lake, a mile around, that is popular with walkers, joggers and bicyclists.

"Right by that lake, a few years ago, some of your people

were pissed off at each other and they started shooting and they killed children. I could have been one of the people who died. I will never vote for you, or any Mexican like you."

He worked himself up to a very nasty tirade. He started calling me a dirty Mexican and told me to go back to my country. "You guys are used to shooting each other but we always have lived peacefully in this country and we don't need your crap," he said. Then he shoved me down the walkway, pushing me, insisting that I should go back to Mexico.

That was probably one of my worst encounters canvassing. It upset me so much, I had to quit for the rest of the day. I cried for a few minutes. Cristy and I hugged each other and we went home.

Now, as I drive past that house, I often wonder if the man has died. He didn't seem healthy, and his attitude certainly wasn't indicative of a sense of well-being. I must confess I occasionally read the obituary column with curiosity, looking for his name. I only hope that with so many wonderful Latinos living in Reno, that this man will read the newspaper one day about a Latino's achievement and that he will have a sudden change of heart. Or maybe something dramatic will happen. Maybe one day a poor Latino kid who plays at Virginia Lake may come to his aid and save his life.

In the end, I knew anger is a form of self-hatred. I had to overcome moments of intense ire during my campaign. Little by little I came to the realization that I couldn't live with so much anger. After all, people had the choice of either liking me or hating my guts, and they might act from their feelings. When you run for office, you expose yourself to other people's self-hatred and fear. You can't expect everyone to like you and be desperately disappointed when they don't if you expect to survive the ordeal. I wasn't representing only Emma Sepúlveda as I walked door-to-door. Like it or not, I did represent the Guatemalan, the Chilean and the Mexican people, rich and poor.

I also understood I represented all the Latinos, including those very few who were "shooting each other." My connectedness to them was something I had to live with and had chosen to live with when I ran for office.

My door-knocking campaign certainly helped me grow. It gave me great insight into the people who constitute what is called the premier democracy in the world. There were many folks who were fair-minded, rational, even passionate about the democratic process. Then there were those who represented the antithesis of democratic thinking. To them, I was just a "beaner," a foreigner trying to get involved in the politics of *their* land. Yet, all that didn't shake me.

What saddened me most was my new sense of how great a role money plays in the politics of this country. With enough financial backing, you need never show up on citizens' doorsteps to introduce yourself and ask for votes. At the same time, so many people of voting age don't even bother to vote. Invariably, the non-voters are deeply affected by the decisions of the politicians who gain office by virtue of having enough money. Too few voters and too much money is a bad combination.

But on the eve of the primary election, in September, after three months of going door-to-door six days a week, my doubts about the strength of American democracy were easily pushed to the back of my mind. I was fascinated with what I was learning about people! I even went door-to-door on election day. Some people would say, "Hey, I just voted for you."

"Well, can you vote for me again?" I'd ask.

I was three months smarter than when I had filed to run for office. But I was still a political neophyte. I was an optimist who believed bringing my campaign to the people could — and would — make a difference.

The Politics of Politics

THE DAY OF THE primary election, I was sky-high.

I knew the Republican challenger in the primary, city bus driver Mario Pucci, was a heavy underdog and stood no chance. Still, I marveled at Pucci's tenacity. In a last-minute rush at the incumbent, he and a handful of supporters had worked the entire weekend in their lonely crusade to get his name before the voters. In the sprawling parking lots of Meadowood Mall, Reno's largest mall, every windshield was fixed with a photocopy of his fliers.

Pucci — a tall, dark-haired, muscular man in his forties — was part Italian and part Native American. And he had tremendous heart. It gave me a sad feeling to think that here was a strong candidate to represent the working class, but he was forced to campaign desperately on his own, with absolutely no money from Republicans. His party had turned its back on him.

At the same time, Pucci's determination gave me a real surge of energy. It prompted me to continue canvassing that weekend and even on the day of the primary, building momentum for the two-month run ahead. I prayed Pucci would make a dent in my opponent's tally. Maybe I would even be able to pick up his votes in the general election.

Early in the afternoon, I went door-to-door until nightfall. Some in my committee said this was a dumb idea. Canvassing the day of the election would confuse the public, they said. Why would I want to solicit votes on the day of the election — when many would already have voted? Indeed, some people gave me funny looks and curtly said they'd already been to the polls. What did I want from them?

I merely replied I was walking door-to-door in advance of the general election.

I could see all those long hours of canvassing was reaping rewards. More and more people, wherever I went these days, knew who I was or at least said I looked familiar and inquired about my identity.

When I got back home, I told my family and supporters I didn't want to hear the voting results. Just keep the early results to themselves.

The next day, I implored people to leave me in the dark. For me, no news was the best news. There was no victory party that night. I simply treated it as another regular day.

It was full speed ahead now.

I stopped by campaign headquarters to sign thank you letters and pick up phone messages to return calls the next morning. Routine business.

My opponent had prevailed comfortably, I was told.

"Now we have to look toward debate preparation," David said. "It's just your opponent and you. From now on it is full steam ahead, because we only have a couple of months."

Full steam ahead? What had I been doing the past three months, going at a snail's pace?

I was told our efforts would have to be redoubled now.

And I knew that, from this moment on, I had to campaign like a fiend. There would be debates, propaganda attacks to fend off, a whirlwind of appearances, impassioned speeches.

The real battle had begun.

The paradox of watching the general election draw nearer every day is that it fills you with great excitement but also with unremitting fear. It is a constant adrenaline rush that robs you of sleep and drains you of energy but also keeps you going at 100 miles per hour, like a speed freak. Not one single day, hour or minute could be wasted. Everything had to be focused on the cause.

The knot in my stomach gripped tightly from the moment I awoke to the moment I nodded off. Yet, I hardly gave it much notice any more.

My disease, lupus, had been in remission for three years. I treated it as if it wasn't even an issue with me, even though I knew that as I depleted my strength in the nonstop effort to get elected I could be putting my health in real jeopardy. I opened the newspaper one morning and saw that a reporter had compared me with my opponent. My opponent was described as "a fitness buff." I was described as the owner of "a chronic disease" marked by extreme fatigue and listlessness, which progresses to death.

This affected me deeply. I was beginning to experience personal and mean-spirited attacks now.

That reporter had called me two days earlier to question me about my lupus. He said that a political consultant (a Democrat!) had given him the news, from my medical records, and that one issue that should be explored in my campaign was my health. Apparently somebody had gotten into my medical records to find some "dirt," as the reporter put it. Could this physically weak woman be elected to office?

That day was one of the lowest and saddest of my campaign. I felt attacked on something against which I could not defend myself. Yes, I do have lupus, and I have done much more in my life than many people who do not have this disease. But what, I considered, would happen if, as I expended every ounce of strength on winning my race, I was suddenly stricken with an outbreak of lupus, had to be hospitalized and died?

The idea of my health deteriorating suddenly, the idea of people getting in my medical records, and the story being plastered all over the news — this sick woman withering away, a casualty of her own political campaign — gnawed at my consciousness.

It was just one more stressor to cope with as the race turned into a sprint.

When I decided to toss my hat into the state Senate race, I drew plenty of funny looks from even those who supported me. More than once I was asked why an honest person of integrity such as myself would want to get into politics.

They made it sound like only the sleaziest of the sleazy got into this game. Others approached me with heartfelt advice: don't get into politics, it's a filthy business and is going to cost you your career, your husband's career, and your life is never going to be the same. Nevada politics just isn't a place for an immigrant yet, not even in 1994, they said.

Some people even expressed that they were taken aback. They had thought I was a straight arrow. They didn't know I was a "politician."

A woman writer in town came up to me at a social event. "I thought you were a poet," she said. "I have read your work and heard you read. You have a soul. Why would you like to sell it?"

After I saw the first mean attack in the newspaper I really wonder if I had what it takes to be an elected official.

If the campaign leading up to the primary had seemed draining, now I had two months where every second had to count. It all boiled down to two considerations: time and money. If I managed each properly, they would equate to election to office come November.

I had to schedule every minute to be spent constructively. I took a reduced salary from the university and taught just one class — the Spanish Practicum course, where students went into the community to use their Spanish as volunteers at hospitals, the courts and anywhere translators were needed. I felt that with the tremendous need in my community I could not stop teaching that class and thereby prevent the volunteers from reaching the Latinos who needed them so much.

I was now caught in a whirlwind, a prisoner of the political process, an everyday game of "beat the clock." I'd awake in the morning, the knot already gripping my stomach, filled with a sense of excited fatigue. Get up. Fix my smile (being a teacher, one becomes accustomed to putting on a happy face), read the newspaper scanning for any negative articles about me and checking out the letters to the editor. Then head off to breakfasts or brunches with lobbyists or interest groups, some of which I hadn't known existed; visit job sites and meet with employees from those in the trenches to the lawyers and executives. Then off to meet-the-candidate functions, where, sometimes, the only attendees were the handful of local candidates, and we would end up hilariously delivering our two-minute spiels to one another for the fourth or fifth time that week.

Despite the madcap treadmill, there were two personal commitments I tried never to fail to work into my schedule. One was taking Jonathan to school in the morning, and spending a few minutes with him in his classroom, because he was petrified something was going to happen to his mother. He was certain that somebody would kill his Mom before Election Day. He would cling to me, pleading with me not to leave him. The other thing I never neglected was picking Jonathan up at 3 p.m. The moment he'd see me out in the hall, his little face would break into a huge smile.

But apart from that, every breakfast, brunch, lunch and dinner (hardly eating anything) I was available to answer questions. My schedule was unremittingly hectic.

Sitting at the table each morning, I'd decide what functions to attend that day. My daily planner calendar became jammed with entries. I'd open it, and it would list dates and times from place to place to place. It got to be so chaotic that my friend, Pam, took over the responsibility of being my driver.

Every minute counted. She'd drop me off near an entrance, knowing that taking time to park the car first could cost precious minutes needed to travel to the next engagement. There were dozens of interviews with the media or organizations considering their endorsements. Everyone wanted to know where each candidate precisely stood on each and every issue. I had to complete hundreds of questionnaires from various interest groups, ranging from animal protection people to a tobacco industry coalition to religious rights groups, conservationists, insurance groups, senior citizens and education organizations.

I ignored the questionnaires from a few extremist groups. One right-wing, anti-abortion association sent propaganda to my home with the picture of a garbage can containing fetuses. My son saw the package and became visibly shocked and upset, and I had to explain to him what it was. I was outraged.

But that's the sort of thing that turns up in the mail when you're running for office.

The campaign kept on getting dirtier and dirtier over the next weeks. One afternoon I was knocking on doors on Nixon Street in the Old Southwest. At one home, a man, a Republican, recognized my face. "Oh, my daughter and some of her classmates at Reno High have been working on your signs," he said.

I must have looked puzzled. "I'm sorry," I said, "I don't have any high school students working on my signs."

But he was certain. "Oh, I overheard them last night saying they were working in this area on Emma Sepúlveda's signs," he said.

I said, "Oh that's nice," and continued on my rounds. On the corner, a sign I had left in a friend's yard was missing.

I knocked on her door. I asked what happened to her sign.

"Some time last night they stole it," she said.

My conversation with the gentleman up the block suddenly took on new meaning.

My friend built up the courage to walk to the man's house with Cristina and me. We knocked.

"I heard that your daughter is part of a high school ring that is supposedly getting paid to 'work' on Emma Sepúlveda's signs," my friend said. "Apparently they 'worked' on my sign last night, because it disappeared."

The man immediately did what police detectives term "turning sideways." "Oh, no, no," he said. "It was a misunderstanding." He said that after I left his house, he spoke with his daughter and learned he had it all wrong. She and her friends had nothing to do with sign-snatching. It just wasn't the case, no no no.

This campaign was changing. Everything that Jan Evans and other people had warned me about was coming true.

Another night, about 3 a.m., I heard noises in the back yard. Sometimes sounds of youth activity from Moana Lane, which runs past the back of our house, carries toward us in the still night air. But this racket was much louder. Like someone banging down a door.

I woke up John. He told me to calm down. I couldn't. I had become so edgy by now that I immediately went into my son's room, whose windows face the back yard. I turned the room lights on.

I heard two cars speeding away.

The next morning, John and I drove around the block. Every one of my four large campaign signs on our back fence had been removed. In their places were a row of my opponent signs and his campaign literature spread all over our back yard.

John stopped the truck practically in the middle of Moana, got out and began tearing down the signs with his bare hands.

This was a personal attack. It was one thing to steal signs from other people's yards, but this vandalism was on our own property!

We made a police report that day.

But I couldn't preoccupy myself too much with responding to those tactics. There wasn't the time; besides, what could you do?

It seemed like there wasn't even time to catch a decent night's sleep. I was getting only four hours a night. Lying in bed, physically exhausted, I found it impossible to turn off my mind and doze off. I'd ponder everything I had said to every group and individual that day, and vow to be better the next day.

I had a new admiration for politicians. Honest, clean, decent politicians. Someone who, for the right reasons, wants to be a public servant is in my mind a true hero. Running for office takes an incredible toll — physically, mentally and emotionally.

Interviews with the media proved very enlightening.

The Reno daily newspaper, the *Gazette-Journal*, sent a young political reporter out. He was dapperly clad in a blue blazer and red tie like a young Republican, and seemed very friendly, but his ideological slant came through in his articles. One time, we spoke for a half-hour over the phone. I mentioned only briefly that my opponent didn't live in the district, and I spent most of my time speaking about the State Industrial Insurance System, what we needed in education, how he never contributed anything to anti-crime legislation and how unreasonable his "one strike you're out" proposal was — playing as it did off of California's "three strikes you're out" rule requiring life imprisonment for those convicted of a third felony.

The following morning, I looked at the newspaper. The headline was: "Foe Attacks Candidate's Second Marriage."

I had never mentioned that he had been married again. My words had been twisted around, and the result was I was being portrayed as a vicious bitch assailing my opponent for marrying a woman who lived in Las Vegas.

My only point — and I hadn't made it a main one — was that I believed the senator should live in the district he represents.

David, my consultant, told me that from that moment on, when the media wanted to get hold of me the interview requests had to go through my campaign staff, and the reporters had to specify what subjects they wanted to cover. It also would be prudent to always have someone from the campaign staff present at any interview.

The newspaper or TV reporters would call me about every other day for responses to local or national news. One of my worst experiences was with one of the reporters of the Reno alternative newsweekly at the time, *The Nevada Weekly*. He was a very negative person, and the tone of his interview revealed his lack of respect for women and minorities. He was constantly trying to trip me up, digging for some sensational nugget he could use to discredit me.

He had previously written an article challenging my opponent's residency in District 4. Now, during our interview, he wanted to return to the topic, while I wanted to move on and talk about myself.

"This will be the first time you've run for office. Have you served on any public bodies such as a commission?" he queried.

"I've been very active in non-profit organizations and community organizations mostly," I said.

"But not political organizations?"

"No. And I find that positive. I don't consider myself a professional politician. And I think I'm probably going to bring a new perspective to some of our problems."

"A lot of people get into politics who might be called 'candidates from nowhere.' They have not participated in any party activities, and then suddenly one day they're running a major state office. They think they have good ideas, and expect to be elected. What have you done to prepare yourself for this office, to be a legislator in Carson City to deal with what you said are very complicated issues?"

"I don't believe anybody gets a degree, you know, in Senate 101 or Assembly 102. I believe you are elected to find out some of the answers to the problems people are facing. I think when you get there, you get the experience."

The interview ran to two hours and the questions were all framed in a similar manner. At the end, he looked at me and said: "You know who you remind me of? The lady in the movie *Havana*."

The daily newspaper proved to be a different story when the time came for the endorsement of candidates.

I went there full of trepidation. I expected it to be a grilling — the editorial board would no doubt find some reason not to endorse me in favor of my opponent.

I walked into the editor's office. There was the executive editor, Ward Bushee, the longtime editorial page editor, Bruce Bledsoe, and a Puerto Rican woman who'd recently been named assistant editorial page editor, María Padilla.

Everybody's questions were good, on the mark. "Why are you running?" "What is your experience?" "What are your issues?" "What do you want to accomplish as a legislator?" "Why do you think you should be elected over your opponent?"

I left their offices with a great feeling, like they really had given me my day in court. These people are not out to nail me, I told myself.

I didn't get their endorsement. But they didn't attack me, either. They backed my opponent, but said I was a great candidate. In the end, the need to keep a Republican majority in the Senate to protect the interests of northern Nevada tipped the scales in my opponent's favor. A great game the Republicans play, reducing candidacies to the politics of geography.

One of my big disappointments in the campaign concerned the students at UNR. I sensed no excitement from them. Complete apathy. Coming from a generation where the university students created the winds of change in politics, I thought I could count on college students to back me as a candidate who would represent them. If anyone knew the problems facing higher education, it was me, not my opponent. I was mistaken in thinking that the students cared about politics. I said as much to the reporter from the UNR student newspaper and he wrote an article including my comments. There was no reaction from the students to the article, either.

The lack of enthusiasm on my own college campus contrasted starkly to feedback I was getting back home. A Chilena journalist based in Washington, D.C., called to interview me as the first Chilena who had become a naturalized U.S. citizen and was running for a state office.

"What an incredible honor for somebody to represent her party," she said.

The balancing act between spending time presenting my message and raising the money to get it out was never more precarious than when I had to decide whether to spend several days meeting with lobbyists and key people in the Democratic Party in Washington, D.C.

It would steal four days from my campaign. But it could prove vital to my fund-raising efforts.

I was going to Washington to attend meetings of the U.S. Senate Hispanic Task Force. The task force's aim was to examine the conditions and realities of Latinos in America. Each state sent at least one representative. I was selected as the only one from northern Nevada. I would be meeting with Senator Reid's chief of staff, a Latino who has worked tirelessly to get Latinos appointed or elected. Throughout my campaign he loomed as a hidden presence, a guardian angel of sorts, helping me as much as he could, as he endeavored to help all Latinos socially or politically.

When I arrived in Washington, he proved instrumental by introducing me to people who could provide me with campaign funding. So did my campaign consultant. David had worked inside the Beltway, writing position papers and reports on environmental issues and the like, as well as orchestrating get-out-the-vote and mailings for certain candidates. He had many contacts. He wanted to be in Washington to show me around. He saw a golden opportunity for me to build up my campaign chest.

One of the first steps for an immigrant who gains U. S. citizenship should be to visit Washington. I had missed it up until now. A friend of David, a lawyer who worked for U.S. Attorney General Janet Reno, picked me up from the airport and gave me the night driving tour, showing off the lights and the darkened monuments. It was very emotional as we passed the White House. It seemed very much like a pilgrimage.

The day I first faced Capitol Hill, teeming with earnest-faced men and women in blue or gray or black suits, clutching brief cases and walking two notches more briskly than normal in and out of doors, I told myself perhaps one day I could be walking up these broad steps in a totally different capacity. I suppose every young politician has those fleeting thoughts.

Outside, knots of reporters and photographers staked out areas, waiting to pounce on unsuspecting sources. David and I entered the domed Senate building, and it seemed as if we had stepped into the Land of Oz. It was like an immense city inside — the subworld of politics. An enchanted world inhabited by deal-cutters, lobbyists and policy-makers. We passed through a metal detector and were quizzed by security personnel about where we were headed. We were going to Sen. Reid's office. We were issued visitor badges and given directions. However, we decided to first visit the floor of the Senate, so we got into a little subway car which shuttles between the buildings.

I glanced around the car. Sitting nearby were two Democrats — Illinois Sen. Paul Simon and New Jersey Sen. Bill Bradley. Such is the instant facial recognition in this era of C-Span and CNN that for a fleeting moment you want to get up and start asking them their opinions on various issues or to volunteer on what votes you've agreed or disagreed with them in the past. I had to consciously restrain myself. I was the only outsider in the car. I could overhear their conversation.

I expected to glean some inside information on crucial votes they had planned. "Which way do you stand on invading Bosnia next week?" Something like that. Instead, they were talking about the weather, where to go for lunch, and where they went last weekend.

I gazed over at Sen. Bradley, a man I've admired for a long time. I had read everything about his life and career. I knew he'd been a star college basketball player at Princeton, a Rhodes scholar at Oxford and then a professional player for the New York Knicks, after which he had gotten into politics and been elected a U.S. Senator from New Jersey. I liked his stance on welfare reform, his defense of affirmative action. He glanced up. Our eyes met.

He stood up and gave me his seat. That little, insignificant gesture proved to me that my high opinion of this man was correct.

It was as close as we got to speaking.

My first item of business was meeting with Sen. Reid. David and I arrived at his offices. His chief of staff, Reynaldo Martinez, was waiting. I had brought along videocassettes of my TV commercials. I was eager for feedback. Martinez is a seasoned veteran of political campaigning. He is a large, athletic man in his fifties, whose father had come from Mexico to work on the railroads. He later moved the family to Las Vegas. In high school he became involved in politics. He helped his good friend, Harry Reid, be elected as student body president. He earned a baseball scholarship to college, then followed his political yen as a behind-the-scenes adviser, eventually accompanying Reid to Washington.

Sitting in his office next to Senator Reid's, I could see that every politician's dream is to have a man (or woman) like this Latino man on his or her staff. He knew the ins and outs on every level of campaigning.

One of his first pieces of advice to me was that I had to take the middle ground. I couldn't wear only the hat of a Latina. "You are going to be elected representing your district, not the small portion of people in your district who happen to be Latino, or any other group, for that matter," he said. "You have to be the candidate who appeals to everybody. So you cannot take an extreme position on any issue."

He had scheduled meetings for me with lobbyists representing industries with special interests in Nevada. They wanted to meet with candidates with political futures. I was to visit with a mining lobbyist, an energy lobbyist, a utilities lobbyist, and several others. David also set up meetings for me. One night, I went out to dinner at a fancy restaurant with two lobbyists hired by the nuclear power industry. They wanted to put a nuclear power plant in Nevada.

The restaurant, according to David, was a typical Washington insider's establishment, full of movers and shakers. Exclusive. The two lobbyists — yuppyish guys in their late thirties, expensively garbed — started drinking and questioning me on my views. Soon, their girlfriends arrived, tall, blond, gorgeous trophies. The wine went around; the meal was all to be charged to the client's credit card. It was a regular party. The most vibrant topic of conversation had to do with some little safety device for reactors that one of the lobbyists made light of. He explained how he was selling it to the power utilities, even though he knew, deep inside, it was hardly fail-safe and could lead to a devastating accident.

He was obnoxious. He was so cynical about his job, he hardly seemed human, much less adult. He launched into his pitch about how beneficial it would be for Nevada to become the nation's first repository for high-level nuclear waste — how it would create jobs, land Nevada lots of federal aid, wean us off our dependence on the gambling industry and lead to unlimited economic growth. At the same time he made it clear that he could never live in Nevada. He keep referring to "you guys in Nevada." I cut him off and said I would oppose every effort his clients made to make Nevada a waste dump, much less a location for a nuclear reactor.

At the end of our conversation, when he realized I wouldn't budge on my views, he said, "Well, you sound so good and you're so good-looking that maybe I'll send you a personal check for your campaign."

I wouldn't have accepted it if he had actually followed through.

I fared much better with the mining lobbyists. For good reason. I consider myself an advocate for mining.

The economies of many South American countries prove that responsible mining is beneficial. Chile has the biggest open-pit copper mine in the world. It is a mainstay of the nation's wealth.

But I was also aware of the terrible conditions under which South Americans toiled in the mines, and how pristine environments could be ravaged. Nevada's mining industry has made a serious effort to recover and preserve the land. And I know how vital it remains for the state, even a century after the Comstock tapped out. Too many restrictions on mining would mean companies pulling out of the Silver State to try their luck elsewhere in the world, where labor is cheaper and environmental laws less strict.

In all, I raised $7,000 that week. It wasn't much considering I raised $130,000 in total during my campaign. But as soon as I returned to Reno, my Washington fundraising became a campaign issue.

My opponent's camp trumpeted that I had received "Washington money," like it wasn't clean.

The U.S. Senate Hispanic Task Force was headed by five
senators from states with heavy Latino populations, including
Harry Reid. The next morning I was to attend the first meeting.

It was about 7:30 in the morning. I stood in the hallway
feeling relaxed and invisible. David was waiting for me at Reid's
office, along with Sen. Reid. The senator greeted me with a warm
hug. We visited for a few short minutes in his office. We were
constantly interrupted by phone calls that he had put on hold.
At the same time the TV screen showing action on the Senate
floor was constantly flickering; if he had to appear on the floor,
he had to know immediately. And he had already been at work
for two hours. It impressed me how hard these senators worked,
unlike the preconceptions many of us entertain about our elected
officials. As early as 8 a.m., his waiting room was filled with
people who needed a few minutes of his time.

Our last meeting with the Hispanic Task Force ended at 7
p.m. Sen. Reid's work day was far from over. He still had several
hours of business left. Then his wife was stopping by. The two
had to attend a cocktail party for foreign dignitaries.

Politics never sleeps.

My trip to Washington proved to be eye-opening. I could
see that Hispanics were gaining power — slowly, to be sure, but
the movement was coalescing and would one day be a political
force to be reckoned with.

I also realized how naive I had been about who really pulls
the strings in Washington on many of the issues. The special-
interest groups — represented by the lobbyists — were the ones
who held the power. These influence merchants crowded the
corridors of Capitol Hill. Still, it had been a thrill to sit in the
office of a U.S. Senator — me, an immigrant from South America
— hashing over serious issues.

My tight schedule in Washington still allowed me the opportunity to meet people for reasons other than fundraising.

I had wanted to meet Sen. Ted Kennedy while I was in Washington. Years before, on a trip back to Chile, I'd seen him delivering a speech in Santiago, in the plaza in front of the Cathedral

downtown. Pinochet had been in power several years by now, and many in the audience had been against Kennedy, because they believed he didn't sufficiently support a return democracy in Chile. Others, the right-wingers, hated him, labeling him a socialist in the government-controlled press. But I had admired his stand on social issues. He was charismatic. Also, hearing him was as close as I could ever get to basking in the aura of his brother, John.

It seems Sen. Reid had mentioned in a casual conversation with Sen. Kennedy that he was meeting with a candidate for state office in Nevada who is originally from Chile. He knew Kennedy had always been interested in Chilean politics.

A young lawyer, one of Reid's aides, arranged the meeting. It was beautiful sunny Thursday morning in Washington. Kennedy wanted to meet outside and chat for a few minutes. I waited in the hall outside the Senate floor. When Kennedy came out, a number of people — reporters and supporters — in the hall descended on him. He was running for re-election in 1994, and running for his political life in a tight race. His once-invincible popularity was in shreds. He even had to mortgage his house to raise extra money in his fight to stay in office.

Sen. Reid called him to the side and introduced us. "Ted, this is my friend, Emma Sepúlveda, the lady who came from Chile and is running for office in Nevada."

Kennedy was rather emotional. He talked about how much Chile had suffered, how wonderful a country it was, what fine memories he had speaking outside the Cathedral. The glint in his eyes showed how much he truly cared about Chile, how sad-dened he was by the thousands who had died after Allende was overthrown. I told him I had been in college at the time.

"Let's go outside, it's such a beautiful day," he said.

Up close, I could see he had been an attractive man at one time. Now, he was getting old and was overweight. He walked with great difficulty, bent over as if he was suffering a great deal of back pain.

"What do you know," I said, "I'm running for political office now in the United States."

His face brightened. "Good for you!" he said.

We stood on the Capitol steps. Kennedy was quite a character, a man who laughed easily, as well as an obvious target of humor. Three Democratic senators stood nearby. They were talking about us, probably wondering who the hell this little Latina was talking to Sen. Kennedy. "What are you meeting about?" one called out.

Kennedy turned around. He cracked a senatorial joke. "Hey, are you guys trying to work up a new health-care plan?"

The senators laughed. "Hey, what are you up to, Ted?" one of them asked.

"Oh, I'm just meeting a candidate for office in Nevada."

"Nevada?!" they said. "A candidate for *what?*"

"For the Senate."

Then he added a very sharp quip. "She is the only candidate in the state who would dare talk to me now."

Kennedy's personal photographer was standing nearby. "I want a picture with Emma," he said.

Then he called out to the senators, again, very loud.

"Hey, you guys look over here. This is the only candidate in the country who will dare take a picture with Ted Kennedy at this moment."

He put his arm around me. *Click.*

Then I began having reservations. Would I return to Nevada and be labeled as some radical supported by Ted Kennedy?

Whatever help he might give me in my campaign, I hoped it would not be public, I told him.

He said he understood. "Why do you think I was joking about you being the only candidate to dare take a picture with me?"

Kennedy and I shared a few more comments about elections. Then I gave him a hug goodbye and said I'd keep in contact. I turned around.

Three lobbyists from Reno were watching us.

I had gotten a taste of the national political machinery. Now I was back in Nevada, cutting my teeth on the local party machine.

I had already met the two U.S. Senators. I had visited with Sen. Richard Bryan early on, before I had even filed for office. We had met at Lyon's restaurant for coffee early in the morning. He was running for re-election and made it a point to shake everyone's hand — the hostess, the waitress, customers — as he walked through the restaurant toward my table.

Bryan was locked in a tough race with a Republican lobbyist. The first time my son saw his campaign ad on TV, he ran into the kitchen and said, "Mom, you'll never believe who's running for the Senate, too! The man from the *Ghostbusters* movie!" I suppose he did bear some resemblance to actor Dan Ackroyd.

Bryan ordered coffee and spoke for several minutes about how wonderful my background was and what incredible things I'd done in my life. I was a strong candidate, he said.

He asked the routine questions — Why did I want to run? What were my positions on the issues? Then he started explaining what a difficult election it was going to be and how little chance I had to win.

He reached into his jacket, took out a pen and started jotting down figures on a napkin. "How many voters in your district?" he asked. "You can't make it for less than $250,000," he said.

Bryan started explaining how impossible it would be for someone like me — someone unknown — to raise that kind of money.

"If you don't raise the money, you don't win," he concluded. I appreciated his advice and honesty. I knew he had his own race to win and he could not help me personally.

My aim now was to meet with Gov. Bob Miller. My opponent had made public in the newspapers that he had paid a visit to Gov. Miller and reminded him of his work on SIIS, and it was now up to the governor to support him as a candidate.

The governor had never come out and publicly supported my candidacy. Some Hispanics in his support line, "Amigos de Miller," began questioning why he hadn't. I was driving to a meeting one day after I'd returned from Washington, and my cellular phone rang.

"Emma, this is Gov. Miller," he said.

How had he gotten my private number?

"I would like to talk to you, Emma, because I have never said that I'm not going to support you. It's the other way around. I support every Democratic candidate and I would like for you to know that I have my own race to win, but I will do everything possible to support you. As a matter of fact, I'm going to take a break from my campaign, and I would like to take you out to lunch. I would also like for our meeting to include Yolanda so we can discuss ways I can help you, and I'd also like the minority leader of the Senate, Dina Titus, to attend."

This was good news. I certainly hoped he could open some doors for me to raise campaign funds.

We had a noon lunch at the Airport Plaza Hotel. I was proud of Yolanda — my old friend from the Mexican restaurant, who used to dip toothpicks in hot sauce before the restaurant opened so we could watch the customers grimace. She was now heading up the state taxation department and I was running for the state senate.

The senator from Las Vegas arrived. So did the governor, alone. He had driven up from Carson and was going to catch a plane to Vegas after lunch. Nevada is probably the only state in the Union where the chief executive can walk into a restaurant alone for a meal.

Miller explained he had his own campaign to tend to, and needed to count on Hispanic support. If I could help with that support, he'd be very happy, he said. He talked about his record in nominating Hispanics to his cabinet, including Yolanda, and a former student of mine from UNR whom he had named to the state parole board, Lupe Gunderson. He also mentioned a couple of judges he had appointed (Judge Mendoza among them, who later went on to the Public Service Commission). The governor said he didn't want this nonsense about my opponent saying the governor was going to support him to go any further.

"It's to my benefit to have a Democratic Senate," he said. "What would you like me to do to help you?"

"I need for you to open the doors to gaming, because it seems to me they're totally closed," I said.

He said he would try to do that.

I also asked if he could add my name to his telephone polling surveys so I could gauge my progress. He agreed. He also said he would "informally" mention my name to campaign donors.

The governor kept his word. He called me a few days later and said to come to his office in Carson City. He had some money for me.

He personally handed me two campaign checks.

For my part, I attended several meetings of Amigos de Miller and urged them to support the governor.

During my campaign months, wherever I went in the state, I always asked the Latinos to support the governor. On election day Latinos voted for Bob Miller.

Not too many Hispanics had made strong bids for elected office in Nevada.

One of my friends, Brian Sandoval, was running as a Republican for the Assembly in my district. He won not because he was a Latino but because he was one of the best candidate running in 1994. Running as a Republican is probably the way to go if you're a minority, because at least then you're appealing to the wealthy white conservative electorate.

A state senator from Las Vegas with a Mexican background, Bob Coffin, was a Latino who had won office as a Democrat. This time out, my opponent had recruited a Latina woman, an immigrant who was a Republican, to run against the Las Vegas senator and even campaigned on her behalf early on, saying, "the senate needs diversity." That was before he found he had a Latina running against *him* for the senate.

There have been several Latino jurists in Nevada, including district court judges Mendoza and Chairez, and Fidel Salcedo, a municipal court judge. Gus Nuñez, a Cuban descendent, became the first Latino on the Reno City Council.

But all in all, Latino candidates have been few and far between. Latinas have been almost absent from the political landscape of Nevada.

As the general election race kicked into high gear, my staff prepared two big fundraisers.

I had $40,000 in my campaign chest. I needed at least $60,000 more, mostly for TV ads and billboards.

My opponent had shelled out $25,000 from his own pocket for his primary campaign (which struck me as very curious — the in-session salary for a state senator is $8,000).

My fund-raisers were strictly grassroot affairs — an art auction and a Brazilian jazz guitarist concert.

"Arts for Emma" would auction off donated works from local artists. Eighty-five artists responded, from painters to weavers to sculptors. I donated an original photograph published in a book and a signed copy of the book.

Musicians volunteered to entertain, and a performance artist showed up with a routine she had prepared for over three months: a dramatic presentation of Emma Goldman, an activist in the early 20th Century. The actress played a woman who arrives with a suitcase, speaks out for immigrants, waves the American flag, and ends the presentation singing, "America the Beautiful."

It was another emotional moment for me. I cried most of the performance.

Four hundred people showed up for the fund-raiser. We raised $5,000.

A month before election day, Romero Lubambo, a Brazilian guitarist who lives in New York and plays with some of the top Brazilian and Caribbean singers, gave a free performance for me at the Musician's Hall. Pam knew him and persuaded him to fly to Reno.

We raised $2,000, after expenses.

I got a final big boost from Sen. Reid. He flew out from Washington and hosted a private cocktail party of friends and supporters. We raised $5,000.

Meanwhile, checks came daily in the mail, in amounts from $5 to $1,000. They came from individuals and from groups that endorsed me, such as the local Firefighters Union, the Peace Officers Association and the School Administrators Association.

The final push was coming.

It hardly seemed possible, but my schedule spiraled up into an even more frenzied pace. It seemed like I was meeting with everyone and anyone now.

One morning, a campaign staffer told me she'd met a lawyer who was a lesbian and who wanted to meet me.

I met with her for coffee at Heidi's, a local pancake house. She wanted to know where I stood on the issues. She struck me as being in the mold of a white conservative woman. I was shocked; people who have suffered discrimination are usually more sensitive about other people's feelings. Where was she coming from?

I talked and talked, running through my stances. Then she turned to my campaign aide — she didn't even face me with this comment — and said, "What do you think about this woman's accent? Can she be elected with that accent?"

I was insulted. It's totally irrelevant to think somebody's accent is going to keep them from being elected. And the same would be true about the color of my skin or her sexual preference.

Needless to say the woman didn't offer me any help. Nor did I ask her for any. I knew that part of my base support came from gay and lesbian groups and her vote or money would not make me or break me.

A breakfast meeting at one particular men's club, a charitable organization, in fact, will always stick in my mind.

I walked in. It was a warm day and I was wearing a skirt that exposed my knees. Wrong move. Rows upon rows of men wore that, "Hey, baby" look. It was intimidating. I didn't know where to sit. I finally found a place at a table. There was silence in the room. A few awkward coughs. Finally, a club officer stood up.

"Well, now that we have Emma here, a good joke comes to mind," he began.

"Hey, you guys. Emma being from South America, and a woman, I just remembered a good one: What is the difference between a terrorist and a woman with PMS?"

Another sensitive man immediately stood up from a table in back with an answer:

"Hey I know that one. . . at least you can negotiate with a terrorist!"

The room erupted in laughter.

I felt like hiding under the table.

So this is how the conservative white male sees me. Not only a Latina, but a woman (with PMS!) who can't handle politics. Just no one to be taken seriously.

I stood up and explained who I was, why I was running and where I stood on the issues at hand.

Their questions were completely unrelated to my stances.

"What do you think about Proposition 187?" someone asked.

They were upset to hear I was against it.

"We have to get rid of those damn wetbacks!" someone said.

"What are you talking about?" I retorted.

"They're taking jobs away from Americans!"

And so on.

Another asked, "What do you think about bilingual education?"

This group supported English only. You come to this country, you shouldn't speak Spanish in public, they said.
They began giving examples of the evils of allowing languages other than English on the streets.

"My aunt was riding the bus downtown the other day and all these goddamn Mexicans were speaking Spanish and she was so upset because you never know if they're speaking about you," one bright mind offered.

It was 7 o'clock in the morning and I was already exhausted!

They wanted to know if, were I elected, I would move to

open the borders to let the "wetbacks" in.

On the matter of health-care reform, I said I would try to protect a woman's reproductive rights.

"I'm not going to pay for an abortion for some fat black pig who has slept with everybody and been pregnant eight times!" someone said.

Another asked me if I supported Clinton.

I said I did and would vote for him again.

They laughed at my answers. I was obviously just the morning's entertainment for them. The only thing that kept me from storming out was my pride.

Then something flashed through my mind. Some of these men had daughters. At least, by appearing before them, I was planting a seed in their minds that one day one of their daughters might wind up in politics. So I told them I was shocked that they had such antagonistic attitudes toward women in politics. "I'm sure some of you have daughters and have dreams for them just like you have dreams for your sons."

They didn't laugh at that.

I was no more Smiling Emma. If I was going to lose this election, I was going to lose with honor.

With honor, integrity and commitment.

Debatable Debates

MY OPPONENT DIDN'T BOTHER going face-to-face with the general electorate or with me for most of his campaign. He didn't have to. Instead of walking door-to-door, he merely relied upon his billboards, TV and radio ads to get his face and name before the public. Such are the privileges afforded by incumbency and a healthy war chest.

But I knew he would eventually have to submit to debating me. It wouldn't look good to duck his opponent. Yet, I wasn't sure I was looking forward to it myself. Truth be known, I was scared to death to debate. I was warned that by going on camera, my ethnic appearance and foreign accent would automatically nullify me as a choice in the eyes of the more conservative voters. I knew the anti-immigrant backlash in 1994 would cost me votes.

In contrast, my opponent projected himself as part and parcel of The Establishment: a white, slick, smooth, professional politician in a three-piece suit, capable of telling the public what it wanted to hear. But not exactly what was on his mind. And there I was: a brown skin woman with an accent, coming from a different culture, representing views the mainstream didn't care to consider — such as the view that putting more criminals behind bars was a short-sighted and ultimately ineffective way to battle crime; but putting more resources into education would steer society on a better course.

I was told that my opponent's clever, even if outrageous, "one strike and you're out" idea to give life imprisonment to first-time violent offenders, playing as it did off the "three strikes and you're out" rule in vogue in California, would curry favor among voters who would allow their fears about crime to supersede their reason.

I told my consultant, David, I didn't want to debate my opponent. He told me that was a bad idea. I was the underdog and had nothing to lose, while my opponent had everything to lose. In the end, I weighed the pluses and minuses and concluded it would be better to be gutsy and take him on. After all, it might prove to be my only opportunity to publicly expose some of his mistakes and vulnerabilities.

The polls were showing him leading me by a margin smaller than veteran observers had expected. In October, a month before election day, he had 34 percent, while I had 30 percent. 8 percent were for minor-party candidates or, "None of the Above," and a shocking 30 percent were undecided. In a race that includes a strong incumbent, to have nearly a third of voters undecided is highly irregular, I was told. Yes, It was a toss-up.

It gave me a lot of hope.

The first debate was to be on Reno's local public TV station, Channel 5, on a Monday, with the taped show airing that Friday night on a two-hour program called, "Candidate's Forum," which would draw a larger-than-normal public TV audience. The moderator was station manager Rosemary Peacock. Dennis Myers, a TV reporter who had closely followed my campaign, would join Peacock in firing questions at us.

The biggest surprise for me was finding out there would be a third candidate on hand. I had heard of the Independent American Party — whose platform was basically founded on a general antipathy toward what members perceived as a Big Government that had usurped their inalienable rights as Americans and children of God. The IAP called for a return to the roots and spirit of the U.S. Constitution. It had fielded a woman candidate to run for District 4, but she hadn't shown up at any of the candidate luncheons or meetings.

She seemed like a pleasant enough lady, a middle-aged, middle-class housewife and mother, certainly not glib and polished when discussing the issues, nor even much versed on any of them. Everything to her — whether it was class-size reduction or reform of the State Industrial Insurance System — boiled down to getting the federal government off the backs of its citizens and re-embracing the Constitution.

Preparation for the debate was very important. In the weeks prior, I spent several hours each day with my consultant and a young professor, Elaine Castel, an expert on debates, hashing through possible questions the panel would toss at us.

Up to now, I had outwardly kept my cool during the campaign. But the day of the debate, I was so anxious I had trouble eating. I had appeared on TV before, on local talk shows and with my own community program on the local Spanish-language station, so the idea of facing the cameras wasn't the problem at all.

The problem was I had to confront my opponent who by now I disliked so much.

I felt incredible pressure to take advantage of this rare opportunity to shed light on his flaws. At the same time, I had heard he was so mean he could stoop to any level to discredit me. My committee told me to expect an attack. Not knowing how he would attack me frayed my nerves.

Would he out-and-out lie about me or my record, or his, and anger me to the point where I might lose my composure? I was sorely afraid of blowing my election chances with an ill-timed outburst.

John, David, Pam, Elaine and I drove to Channel 5's studios, crammed into a corner of the old Education Building on the University of Nevada campus, for the taping of the debate. My opponent wasn't there yet. We sat in a small waiting room outside the tiny production studio. Channel 5's camera crew was filming other candidate debates. We could follow them on a little monitor in the waiting room. The debates didn't seem so tough. I began to feel calmer.

I was wearing a conservative gray two-piece skirt and blazer and a simple pearl necklace and earrings so my jewelry wouldn't glint in the lights. My hair hung in a tame, straight style and I wore very little makeup so my face wouldn't shine in front of the bright lights. I felt as prepared as I could be. I tried to let my mind go blank.

A woman I recognized as a member of the Republican party walked into the room. She sat across from me. We struck up a conversation. It turned out that, despite her party affiliation, she was no friend of my opponent.

"You have nothing to worry about," the woman said. She labeled him a "puppet."

"I can't stand your opponent," the woman said. "I'm going to give you a tip. One thing that makes him nervous as hell — and I know this because we're in the same party and often in the same social gatherings — if you really want to rattle him during the debate, stare at his funny looking hair."

I told her I appreciated the inside information, but I couldn't imagine myself using that tactic.

About five minutes later, my opponent showed up. With him were two assistants — a young man I recognized as his faithful gofer, and a woman toting a big plastic bag.

His face was already so caked with makeup it gave me the urge to rush to the bathroom to make myself up more. I realized I would look so pale compared to this bronze-looking, shiny-visaged creature.

He immediately strode over to shake my hand. "I wish you the best of luck," he said, gratuitously. As he spoke, my eyes fixed on the gobs of makeup and hair spray plastering his head. I had a hell of a time keeping a straight face. In his gray double-breasted suit, monogrammed shirt, expensive foreign shoes, Rolex watch, gold cufflinks, diamond pinky ring and overpowering cologne, he resembled nothing more than a model portraying a slick politician, sprung straight from the pages of *Gentleman's Quarterly*.

I couldn't have dreamed of a better antidote to my anxiety than this comical figure.

Shortly after, the producer poked her head in and told us to prepare to take our positions. As if on cue, my opponent's female aide popped opened the plastic case, and he bent over so she wouldn't get any makeup on his suit. She proceeded to brush even more brown powder on his face and applied even more gloss to his lips.

This man was seriously concerned with his appearance.

My apprehension over going *mano a mano* with my opponent further dissipated when I saw there would be a third debater.

Just before we were to go on, she showed up wearing a simple cobalt blue dress. The producer ushered the three of us in. Our standing arrangement in front of the cameras further quelled my qualms. The women was positioned at the middle podium, I was on the left and our opponent on the right facing the cameras. With this lady as a buffer, it immediately eased the tension.

I stood on a little platform to elevate me above the podium and put me on an altitude with my opponents. I balanced myself, hoping I wouldn't make a misstep and fall off during my speeches. I reviewed in my mind my opening and closing statements. I glanced at my notecards. I was so prepared I had a little portfolio with index cards on many topics, including handily referenced statistics. I realized I had overprepared, just as I had studied exhaustively for tests in college. I had tried to be ready for any and every surprise.

I could not believe myself. Now, surprisingly, two thoughts dominated my mind: attack him, attack him, attack him; and, look at his hair, look at his hair, look at his hair.

Like a mantra, these thoughts psyched me up and focused me. I was no longer afraid. I felt relaxed and confident. I glanced at my opponent.

He looked preposterous!

He gripped his podium. I noted his hands. His fingers were pink, perfectly trimmed, the cuticles peeled back and the white crescents gleaming. The perfect french manicure! I couldn't suppress a twinge of pity deep inside. Was this debate — this race, even — this important to him? He was a study in insecurity. I could sense his pain. It was a false identity he had wrapped and

enveloped himself in — the made-up, pretentious politician trying to portray perfection, to be cool and in control, yet utterly
uncomfortable in the spotlight. Here, at this moment before the
lights and cameras, I read his nervousness. He radiated self-con-
sciousness, an actor in rehearsal, as if every eye were glued on
him. In a gesture I'll never forget, he suddenly shifted his right
hand slowly from the podium and placed it in his pocket in
what he must have thought was a posture conveying distinc-
tion.

I suddenly felt very sad for him. What was I doing, trying to
destroy his world that he had so painstakingly built up over the
past twelve years?

How could I attack this poor guy? Being a state senator was
his identity, all he had. Why else would he go to such extremes
to prep and primp to defend his incumbency, a job that paid all
of $8,000? I had my life, my family, my writing, my university
career. If I fared poorly in this debate, so what? For him, though,
it seemed a life-or-death situation.

The bank of studio lights flashed on. They were so blinding
and hot that my opponent's makeup began to clot and run. His
features began to resemble a melting candle. He sweated beneath
the perfectly motionless weave of his blond-gray-spray hairdo.

He was dissolving before my eyes. The Betty Crocker cake
of his face was disintegrating.

Three different cameras trained on us from across the room.
The producer explained which one to look right into as we spoke.
An assistant clipped tiny microphones under our coats. The producer went over the thumb's-up cue the cameramen would use
as signals for each of us to begin or wrap up our speeches and
responses. As soon as the moderator would say our time was up,
we would be cut off.

I could hardly see the moderators sitting at a table right in
front of us, because of the light's white glare. It seemed unreal,
as if we would be responding to a machine's questions. It made
me uneasy.

The format would have 90 seconds of opening remarks from

candidates, followed by three questions to each of us from the two-person panel, then closing remarks from the candidates. We wouldn't be allowed to ask each other questions. As the camera lights finally came on, my adrenaline kicked in.

He was first in line to make an opening statement.

His angle in addressing his camera allowed him to catch me out of the corner of his eye. He could glimpse me, and was fully aware I was staring at his hair. He didn't like it. It was like a little game. How could I upset him, and how difficult would it be for him to ignore me?

He said he was running on his record. Instead of using the first person and singular "I," he used the royal "we." "We have supported more than 90 bills relating to crime in the past session," he said. "We" had given education support for class-size reduction, and in the 1980s, "we" had worked to control costs in hospitals.

He was proud of what "we" had done to create a consumer advocacy for lower utility rates. He wrapped up by saying his campaign had everything to do with maintaining Republican control of the Senate to serve the best interests of northern Nevada. In the 1991 session, with Democrats in control of the state senate, southern Nevadans had forced the north to pay its "fair share" of revenues for law enforcement, and it had stretched northern budgets, he reminded.

The last time Republicans didn't have a majority in the Senate, "it cost northern Nevada $9 million," he said. And he took the opportunity to attack State Sen. Dina Titus from Las Vegas.

"This race has to do with the quality of life in northern Nevada."

That did it for me. The pity I felt before dissolved into anger at his misrepresentations of his record. His remarks were like a blessing to my ears. "Yes!" I thought. He had left himself wide open for attack.

I had written down in notes for my closing remarks that he had never introduced a single bill having to do with public safety; what's more, he was one of only four senators who had voted against class-size reduction. I knew I would have the opportunity to zing him.

The other candidate was next in line for her opening statement. Speaking slowly and woodenly, she began. "I'm here as a lay person who's made a personal study of what's going on in our government locally and federally, and I've become alarmed at the trends in our government, particularly in the moving away from Constitutional statutes and fundamental laws.

"Our legislators locally and in Big Government have decided to move away from the Constitution. We need an educated electorate, those who see that government is manufacturing its own laws out of thin air. We need legislators who decide and enforce only natural rights and take none of them from us. We need to remember who gave us our life, liberty and prosperity.

"Is it the bureaucrats and legislators? Or is it God? The Constitution is our shield against tyranny."

She rattled on about family values and other buzz phrases, and how neither the Republicans nor the Democrats had any solutions to the problems facing the country, while "confusion and trickery and lies are reigning and this is what people are frightened about."

Now it was my turn. I had practiced my speech over and over. It seemed to flow easily, though I spoke slowly and tried to enunciate clearly.

"This election is all about the future," I said. "Who is the best person to serve our state into the next century? It is about forsaking the politics of the past. It is about looking into the future to provide our young people the best environment possible to achieve success.

"This country and this community have given me wonderful opportunities, for which I am grateful. I will work to ensure our future generations are given the same opportunities that were given to me. My agenda is simple, straightforward and meets the challenges facing northern Nevada.

"First, I will work to improve our education system. I will support vocational training and do everything possible to reduce class-size, which is among the highest in the nation. Secondly, I will tackle head-on the ever increasing problem of violent crime. I will support tougher sentencing and increase badly needed resources for law enforcement.

"Third, I will work to restore integrity in our government. I will fight for term limits to weed out professional politicians and I will also work to reform the way we finance campaigns. For too long, those with the money have controlled the public agenda in this state, and that needs to change.

"Working together, we will provide our community with the voice of integrity and commitment."

I was first on the list for the panel's questions. Dennis Myers' query threw me; I hadn't expected it and didn't even grasp it at first. He said some open-government advocates, particularly the citizen's group Common Cause, were nervous about my possible election because they'd had problems with educators abiding by the open meeting law, and there were already several educators in the legislature.

I completely misunderstood him and went off on a tangent about my background in education. "Our educational system is in crisis, and I think I will make use of my experience as an educator when we come across bills that need that experience," I said.

I went on about the need for vocational education.

"For too long in this state, high school has been a terminal degree and these students are not prepared to enter the work force."

Myers paused, then said: "I'm not sure we got at the issue that I raised there."

He repeated the question.

"I think I will probably be in favor of open meetings," I said, curtly.

My opponent had his officious answer all ready. "I think you'll find the Legislature in this state is far more open than any other legislature in the country. It's the way it should be, we are the people's legislature and it behooves all of us to support any

open government legislation and to continue to keep it open."
Myers put him on the spot and asked him to clarify.

"Senator, virtually the first thing you did during the last legislative session was close a meeting to the public."

He said he didn't recall that incident. "But we've had open hearings in our meeting process ever since I've been there, since I've been chairman, which I believe has been four terms," he said, without specifying he was head of the Senate Commerce and Labor Committee.

The other candidate also supported open meetings.

"That's one of the issues that independent Americans are really intense on opening," she said, "because the very loss of our rights is directly related to those matters that the public is not aware of." And furthermore, for the public not to be mere "cattle," as "referred to by some government officials," the legislative people should be willing to teach the public so the voting public can become true Republicans and everyone can be a statesman or stateswoman, she said.

Rosemary Peacock raised the issue of how important it was for the Republicans to maintain a senate majority to protect northern interests. My opponent reiterated that losing it would mean southern Nevada exercising clout in allocating funds.

When it was my turn to answer — I pounced.

"It's amazing to me that my opponent speaks so forcefully about keeping the power from going to southern Nevada, when we know he spends most of his time in Las Vegas. It's a real conflict for me, because I think he is taking the power to Las Vegas right now."

He was visibly angry at this jibe. I could see him out of the corner of my eye. His face looked furious.

Dennis Myers followed up, asking me why I had a problem with commuter marriages, which were somewhat common in Nevada.

"If you're going to represent a district," I said, "you need to live in that district, you need to have your kids go to school in that district, you need to go to the grocery store in that district, you need to talk to people in that district and find out what problems most concern them. I don't think you can be a part-time senator."

His turn came.

""Everyone in this community knows I've never been a part-time senator," he said. "I've given 110 percent. I've lived in this community close to 25 years, I shop in this district. I do fill up my car with gas. During the session I come home every night, I don't stay in Carson City, just for that purpose. To get to know my constituents. So they can complain to me. So they can articulate their problems."

He ended by saying he spent most of his time in the county.

It was time for our closing statements. The IAP candidate went first. "For me, family is first and family needs are directly connected to taxes and crime," she said, and carried on about the need to disconnect ourselves from federal government "via subsidies, mandates, whatever, so we as Nevadans can be a whole state and be regulated from within." Also, families needed lower taxes "so that they can function as a family while teaching their children at home, hopefully, the traditional American values" and we won't have gangs and career politicians, but, instead have a constitutional republic.

It was my turn.

I thanked Channel 5 for letting voters have a chance to see the real difference between my opponent and myself. He represents the politics of the past, while I represent the politics of the future, I said.

" He has said he's going to be tough on crime. However, for 12 years he did not introduce a single bill related to crime. My opponent, where have you been for 12 years? Have you just now discovered that your community has a serious problem with crime?"

The same is true with education, I said. He was one out of only four senators to vote against class-size reduction. "My opponent, where have you been for 12 years? The community deserves a full-time senator. The choice is clear: a career politician who has spent his entire career thinking about his next election, or a voice of integrity and commitment that is thinking about the next generation."

Now it was his turn.

"Where I've spent my time for the last 12 years is on Commerce and Labor, where I've chaired it for the majority of that time, trying to protect you against utility increases, trying to protect you against increases in health care costs, trying to protect you against unnecessary increases in your automobile insurance," he said.

His voice began to weaken, like he had a frog in his throat.

"My position on crime is well-defined," he said. "I believe in one strike you're out on violent crime, and I think the next session of the Legislature will address that. The health-care issue is so critical, and the cost of Medicaid could in fact eat up our whole budget. They're tough issues, and they need tough leadership, and I hope I can continue that in Senate District 4. Thank you."

And with that our debate was over.

It seemed like 15 minutes had flown by. It left me with the feeling I hadn't said anything I'd wanted to say, there hadn't been an opportunity to really debate.

The cameras turned off, the lights flashed out. I shook hands with the other candidate. The senator for District 4 was in no mood for this, though. He was clearly annoyed. He shook hands with Dennis Myers anymore. What an actor! I was abhorred. How he could stand in front of the cameras and posture and pontificate about his voting record. In 12 years of political service, all he could boast of was having formed a consumer advocate's office — when he had been a Democrat, no less! — and about SIIS reform, the ultimate outcome of which remained unclear.

My initial pity for him had now turned to pure anger. For his part, I was sure he was fully aware of how much I disliked him. The enmity between us had now been defined.

John and my friends were waiting for me outside.

I had a good feeling, but I believed I could've done much better.

The next debate was a real debate. The format was set up so that we could grill each other.

The local chapter of the Soroptimists International — one of the best groups of professional women in our community and extremely in tune with civic and social matters — organized the luncheon event in a conference room of a downtown hotel-casino. There was a large noontime audience, and the TV and print media showed up to cover it.

The debate was to be longer than the fleeting 15 minutes at Channel 5. Each of us would make opening remarks at a podium, then field questions from each other as well as from the audience. The third candidate had not been invited. It was just he and I.

I felt even more nervous than before the first debate. In fact, I threw up repeatedly that morning. I simply couldn't hold any food in my stomach. My opponent's staff, I'd been told, had scrutinized my life inside and out. His supporters would be in heavy attendance. What vicious and shameful questions had they prepared for me?

Two weeks before the debate, I had received a call from a newspaper reporter who said he was giving me the opportunity to respond to allegations levied against me by a source he would only identify as "a Democratic consultant." The reporter said he had been informed that my father was a "Marxist Communist leader in Chile."

I started laughing.

"Daddy is dead, and he's probably tossing around in his grave thinking that somebody could call him a Marxist Communist when in his own eyes Reagan is too liberal."

"Well," the reporter said, "there's also a rumor that your son isn't attending school in your district, but that you've sent him overseas to go to school." He said the proof of that was that my son spoke Spanish on our answering machine message.

"Well, that is very simple to answer," I said. "You can trace his schooling very easily. He went to Merry Berry for pre-school and he has been at Caughlin Ranch for kindergarten and first grade. He is only 6 years old. How old would he have to be to be sent overseas by himself?"

"Well, he speaks Spanish," the reporter continued.

"Yes, I'm very proud of the fact my boy speaks two languages and doesn't have an accent in either language," I said.

Then he questioned whether my son had been born in the United States. He also added a question about my son's green card.

I told him I could prove I was telling the truth. He could come by my house and I'd show him Jonathon's birth certificate (from Saint Mary's Regional Medical Center) and school records, as well as pictures of my father standing with Pinochet and Dad's campaign literature that spelled out extremely clearly his right-wing politics.

It was obvious to me from this interview that my opponent's camp was busy digging up more dirt on me. And this didn't bode well for the coming debate. At least with the newspaper reporter I had been given a chance to set the record straight. During the debate, it would be his word against mine.

I was so nerve-racked in the hours leading up to our showdown, I realized that my hostility for my opponent was manifesting itself as a physical condition. He literally made me ill. At the same time, I knew I had to keep my temperament under control. I couldn't come across as a negative campaigner attacking my opponent gratuitously — even if I could hardly stand to look at him by now.

My consultant had also heard how my opponent's people were investigating my life with a fine-toothed comb. I think David was even more nervous than I was that morning. He drove over to pick me up and drive me to the debate.

I had thrown up so much that morning I believe I had even retched away the perpetual knot in my gut. But my anxiety remained at high pitch. Then, when we went to get into my truck, we suddenly realized we had locked the keys inside the house!

We had no portable phones to call John to race over and let us in, or even alert the debate organizers of our predicament. We were already running late. Would we now miss the entire affair?

We walked around the house's exterior. In back, I spotted a narrow window cracked slightly open. One of us would have to be hoisted up and crawl through. David is not a slim person. I decided I was too dressed up to go through the window. David would have to squeeze through as best he could.

He pulled himself up. Halfway through, he got wedged in the window. His butt wouldn't allow him progress. His legs wiggled frantically. He was stuck fast. Worse, John and I keep chickens at our house and their poop defaced the window ledge. I pushed David's butt as hard as I could. Finally, with an incredible explosion, I shoved his butt through the window. He dashed to the front door and opened it and I bolted inside to hunt down my keys.

I located them on the kitchen table. We turned to leave. Then I caught sight of David's pants. The seat was befouled with chicken excrement! I was faced with a decision: do I tell this man he had to change his clothes — and we'd end up seriously late for the debate? — or do I ignore it and let my consultant show up with me, his clothes covered in chicken poop? I considered that my opponent's people are always dapperly attired in their three-piece suits. But we had no time for fashion parity. I decided against informing David of his dirty laundry. He would have to find out for himself when he went home. There just wasn't time now.

On the way, it seemed like we were heading to my execution. What gave me extra remorse was that I knew a number of my friends and steadfast supporters had bought tickets to the luncheon and would be in attendance. I had to do my best for their sake as well as defend myself as I was being verbally savaged on stage.

They would cry for me while others would be jumping up

and down, frenzied by the lynching.

When we arrived, the room was packed. A number of people unable to find a vacant seat were standing in the back of the room. I had plenty of supporters in the gathering. But I saw that my opponent's people had two tables full of his staff — aides, consulting firm members — strategically positioned in the front row. I recognized some of their faces. There was his blond, good-looking male lackey who accompanied him everywhere. He seemed very attached to his boss. He looked at me and seemed to smirk with anticipation.

This show of force for my opponent apparently had instructions to keep their eyes fixed on me throughout the debate. His campaign assistants had also brought a video camera to film the debate. This wasn't intended to record the debate for posterity's sake, as it turned out. They wanted to catch a sound bite of me for use in a radio ad, so that everyone would be able to hear that I had a foreign accent.

We refused to acquiesce to letting them tape my appearances at the podium. It was not part of the contract we had signed. This did not deter them from their plan, however. Some of the women, we later learned, had concealed tape recorders in their purses. One woman opened her purse to get her cellular phone and I caught sight of her recorder inside. It made me edgy.

The seating arrangement at the front had my opponent on one side of the podium and I on the other. The Soroptimist chapter president, the debate moderator and the program emcee also sat at the front.

Unlike the first debate, my state of mind remained in turmoil as the moments ticked by and the start approached. He had arrived before me. As I took my seat, he immediately came up, shook my hand, sat next to me and confessed that he was feeling quite ill.

"This is the worst day for me," he said. I believe he was as nervous as I was. "I have the flu and an incredible fever," he said. "I feel very weak. I thought about canceling this but, y'know, I think it's important for us to be here one more time."

I didn't buy any of it. He was incredibly gussied up, about on the scale of the previous debate. All that was different was his gabardine beige slacks and black double-breasted jacket, replacing the more formal gray suit he'd worn before. He still had the monogrammed dress shirt, the cufflinks, Rolex watch and pinky ring. But he wasn't done up as slickly as before. His coiffure seemed to have been sprayed much earlier in the morning; by now it was stiff and opaque and full of dust. Still his lips glistened with pink gloss, and eye shadow touched up his face amid the tons of brown pancake.

He continued to small-talk with me. He asked me about university issues. "How do you think the university is coming along?" he said. He wanted to know how I thought the university was handling the state budget cuts, and what I made of the administration. He was clearly unsympathetic to the university and seemed to want me to confirm his views. I didn't. I had been warned that he didn't support the university because he had never succeeded in getting a job there. He was fishing for criticisms of the campus, but I didn't oblige.

He kept interrupting our chat to blow his nose violently. Every time he wiped it, the tissue would come back covered in dark makeup. He looked at me and said, "I've been using so much Kleenex that I'm sure the paper stocks are going up. I should call my broker in New York to tell him to buy more shares."

I laughed at his quip. He looked taken aback.

"I'm serious, I am going to call my broker," he said.

I stopped laughing. This was certainly bizarre. Was this guy for real?

The debate was to follow lunch. People left their tables for the buffet line. It was simple fare — green salad, canned corn, fruit, soup and the like. I came back with my plate. He did not have any food.

"Aren't you going to eat anything?" I asked.

"I would not dare eat this kind of food," he said.

It wasn't good enough for him.

For a second I entertained making light of this in the debate. Some catty comment like: "Too bad we didn't have lobster today to please my opponent's high-brow palate."

I had my own troubles, though. I worried I would throw up whatever I ate on my plate. I hadn't digested anything that day. I was still frightfully nervous and my heart rate had remained accelerated above normal the entire morning. I had a valid physical reason not to eat. But after his arrogant comment I wanted to demonstrate to him that I was a normal person and would eat what everyone else was eating even if I had to run to the bathroom every few minutes.

I picked at my food and sipped on a 7-Up and an ice tea, hoping to keep myself hydrated. It was funny. After all the campaigning, all the intense lobbying and going door-to-door and hammering signs into front yards and all the preparation for this debate — my goal at that very moment was elemental indeed: If I could get through this debate without throwing up in front of everybody at the podium, I would be very happy, indeed.

I was getting another educational dose of political reality. This game was incredibly rougher than a casual observer could ever imagine.

But even this knowledge didn't make me appreciate my opponent any better. I had witnessed how he had debated me the first time, delivering slick, pat answers. I had watched great debates. I had admired the emotion Bill Clinton had infused into his rhetoric during his campaign debates for president. I had seen, in 1988, Democratic vice-presidential contender Lloyd Bentsen debate his Republican counterpart, Dan Quayle — a classic.

I had seen so many politicians who spoke from the heart. My opponent wasn't one of them. He had only served to confirm for me, slowly but surely, that anyone who has the money and can hire a political machine could get elected. For me, he represented the worst our political system offered as the century drew to a close. He was something I never wanted to become.

For this second debate we were given one minute for opening remarks, then allowed three questions each, and then given another two minutes for closing remarks. The rules also called for the audience to ask questions of candidates during the question-and-answer period.

The moments ticked past in a hurry. I considered that in a live debate you are not only open to attack from your opponent, but from anyone who may be planted in a room with the sole objective of asking you a question that would expose you to the worst public embarrassment of your life. I looked at the rows of tables right in front of me. Who among this gathering were the assassins?

Likely, they were seated in my opponents' section — the two tables practically facing me.

But it turned out their scheme was not to lob grenade-questions at me, but rather to feed juicy pitches to their man to hit over the fence.

In good time the emcee introduced us. The half-hour debate was ready to begin.

There was no coin toss to see who went first with opening remarks. A woman stood up in the audience and said, "Ladies first!" So I got up.

This election is all about the future, I said. Who is the person who can lead our state to meet the problems of the 21st century?

He had no notes written down. On his turn, he basically reviewed his record in office. He always had trouble — or feigned to — in remembering how many years he had served.

"I've been elected, let's see, how many terms?" He'd pause to consider. "Oh, I think this is my fourth."

Then he launched into his familiar North vs. South spiel, about how vital it was he be returned to office to maintain the Republican plurality in the Senate as well as his seniority on key committees, so that southern lawmakers wouldn't gain the upper hand and screw the North out of funds.

His front-table coterie greeted his speech with roaring applause.

Now it was my turn to ask him a question. As I stood at the podium, all eyes from his tables fell upon me in unwavering scrutiny.

"How are you going to be the senator of District 4, when your home is in Las Vegas, your BMW (and this drew laughter from the crowd) is registered in Vegas, and you don't have any attachment to this community? Why are you still running for election from this district?" As I sat down, he shot me the same pissed-off look he'd had when I'd asked this question during our first TV debate.

He stood up, immediately switched to a beaming grin for the audience, and took to the podium.

"Everybody knows that I live in this community, that I have lived in this community since 1976, that I have gone to school here, that I own property here, that I have been married here," he said. "And I still live here. I'm one of the few legislators who doesn't stay over nights in Carson City during the legislative session. I drive back each night to Reno to my home in this district."

He totally glossed over his residency in Las Vegas. Then he really stretched the truth.

"The problem is that my wife and my child live in Las Vegas so, like in many marriages, I have to commute. I spend most of my time here, and I bring my wife here, and we accommodate our lives according to the needs of the people who elected me."

His first question for me was on health care. He wanted to show that he had answers to health-care problems, while I did not.

He asked me whether I knew anything about Access Nevada.

I explained I had lived in countries with socialized medicine, and found that such systems didn't work. My biggest concern on this issue was that we would accept some quick-fix, when what we needed was a long-lasting solution, especially in a state with the highest percentage of uninsured residents and where the cost of decent medical care is among the highest in the nation.

I concluded by saying that if he had the answers to what could be done to help the state's residents, why hadn't he solved the problem in his 12 years in office?

My second question was calculated to arouse indignation among the predominantly female audience. Why was he one of only four senators to vote against allocating $160,000 for the Women, Infants and Children program, thus depriving these vulnerable citizens — low-income pregnant women and mothers who were living slightly above the poverty level of the welfare rolls — of assistance to pay for needed food?

And why, after that vote, had he voted for money to upgrade the computer equipment in legislators' offices?

He completely dodged the question. He said the state has a lot of needs and he was very sensitive to the needs of children and had shown his support of their needs. He pulled out a booklet by a women's rights lobbyist and read what sounded like an informal endorsement of him because of his pro-choice stance.

In truth, it hadn't been an endorsement. It was merely a lobbyist spelling out where each candidate stood. A professional politician, however, need not be concerned with such distinctions.

When questions were opened up to the floor, a woman I did not recognize raised her hand. She stood up and asked him: "Give us a yes or no answer: Did you vote against the $160,000 for the WIC program?"

He was silent for a moment. He prepared to talk, then stopped. Then he looked at her and said, "I voted against the program."

The woman stood up again. "Why did you do that?" she demanded.

"Well, to tell you the truth, I'm not in favor of solving big problems with small solutions," he said. "And I didn't think that was a good request because it wasn't enough to solve the problem of hungry children."

The woman was not appeased. "Good, " she said. "It's better then to give zero money for this program, so they all go hungry by not having food in their stomachs?"

This brought loud applause.

It was a moment I still cherish.

His second question for me was (and I fully expected this one) what would I do to reform the State Industrial Insurance System? It was a truly sneaky question. If anyone — including himself — had figured out how to make this bankrupt state bureaucracy solvent, they would have done so long ago. The truth was, SIIS was probably unsalvageable.

No one had solutions. I said I didn't, either. But I did have many concerns. I said I felt very uncomfortable with the inability of injured workers to choose which physician they want to see. I also didn't like having the period to retrain for a new skill shortened by the SIIS bailout program.

"I'm concerned about some of the reforms that you have made," I said to him. "They have basically produced two results: You have favored "Big Business" and the casinos and reformed SIIS on the backs of injured workers. I'm not about to do that."

My third and final question to him was about crime. Why had he been in the Legislature for 12 years and never introduced or spoken on behalf of a bill to curb or stop crime, yet now he was talking a good line about solving our crime problem. "You didn't do anything, and now you're not even supportive of 'three strikes and you're out.' "

I turned to look at him. "With your new approach of 'one strike and you're out,' we're all going to end up in jail next year."

This drew tremendous applause. I remember looking at the Washoe County district attorney. She was beside herself with mirth. Even he smiled.

His response portrayed me as an idiot.

"As you probably do not know, I'm not on the Judiciary Committee so I cannot introduce bills to stop crime. But my voting record is very positive in support of legislation to fight crime."

His third question for me was also about crime. "How are you going to solve some of our crime problems?"

I said I would ask for a more proactive approach to crime. I did not want to see more drug prosecutions using up our limited jail space. But I was for truth in sentencing, that 20 years should mean 20 years, and that violent criminals should be put in special programs to pay back communities for their room and board.

"Let's stop building prisons and explore alternative sentencing," I said.

The floor was opened to the audience.

His supporters tossed out juicy questions for him. One asked about the consumer advocacy position he had started when he was a Democrat. "Oh let me tell you about that," he said, and went on and on about it.

Another asked whether he was going to increase taxes. "Oh, I have never been for increasing taxes," he said. "We have enough revenue. We just have to find ways to spend the money better."

The debate ended.

I had survived it without puking. But I felt bad.

I believed he had achieved some of his objectives — to show he was experienced and deserved to be re-elected because experienced legislators were called for at this point in time, not newcomers finding their way.

But I had accomplished something, too. I had exposed several of the many weaknesses in his voting record. Thus, I felt quite positive. A number of women who greeted me afterward said I'd done better than my opponent.

Then a Latina women, a good friend of mine, came up to shake my hand. "You know Emma?" she said, "I was talking to a lot of women at my table and they were not very happy with you."

"Why?" I said.

"Well, I'll talk to you later."

"No," I said. "I'm in the aftermath of my debate, I need to know what I did wrong."

"Well, they felt you went too much on the attack. People wanted to hear more about what you're going to do, not what he did wrong."

I was disappointed.

"Well," I said, "I have spent months telling people why they should vote for me. It's about time that I told them why they shouldn't vote for him."

But her comment lingered with me. It darkened my mood on the drive home.

This town was so conservative that even some of the liberal women felt it was not a woman's position to be a candidate and speak negatively against her opponent. What did they want from me — to say everything was wonderful and I'd be just another great candidate?

I felt awful about this. I wanted these women to realize I was running for my life and I needed to attack him and expose him in front of them for what he has not done.

I was supposed to be ladylike about this?

Threats, Tallies, Freedom

BY THE FIRST OF November, the emotional rollercoaster of the campaign had taken me through great and exhausting vicissitudes. It had brought on the intoxicating high of standing in front of a group of supporters chanting, "Emma! Emma! Emma!" as well as the mortifying low of being vilified on strangers' doorsteps because of my accent and skin color. It had buoyed me up with the sweet righteousness of pushing forward a progressive platform to better the lives of struggling and disenfranchised residents who were practically invisible and voiceless. And it had buried me with the bitter frustration of watching an elitist, opportunistic opponent rack up votes purchased with the power of an entrenched party machine.

But a campaign never involves just one emotion at a time. Conflicting feelings often come into play. You believe in yourself as anointed by fate and circumstance to assume the mantle of public office, and at the same time wonder at what moment you will be exposed for something you never did and lose all your support. You commiserate with your opponent at the very instant you wish to destroy him politically. You feel like your run for office has picked up steam and you're charging full-speed ahead, just when you seriously ponder whether to call it quits. This is one of the most glaring paradoxes: a candidate's dogged optimism coupled with a deep fatalism.

Then there are the chronic thoughts you try to submerge deep in your subconscious, cognizant that if they break free into the foreground of your mind they will detonate your will to carry on to election day. One such thought that persisted throughout my run for office was a lingering sense of dread that would ebb or well up from week to week, day to day, hour to hour.

It was the fear for my family's safety and my own safety. The reality of politics in 1990s America is that dirty tactics are as accepted as the beanball in professional baseball. Perhaps those who incorporate such tactics into their campaign strategies rationalize that "everyone" uses them.

And so it was that before I had even filed to run, I had received the anonymous phone calls at home and work asking whether I was "the dumb fucker that wants to get into politics," and calling me one of those "goddamn foreigners" trying to run the lives of Americans.

There had been the caller who warned I would be killed if I filed for office. And then Jonathan had run into my bedroom that afternoon when I'd brought him home from school, hit the answering-machine playback button and heard the death-rattle of a choking person.

The calls had stopped immediately after I'd filed. But they had demonstrated to me how high the political stakes were for some people, even at the state level in little Nevada. And my fear of what such minds were capable of doing stayed with me the entire campaign. You are only human. In all honesty, you can never forget the threats. They change you.

I'll never forget the face of my little Jonathan when he'd heard the strangling sounds on the answering machine. The fear in his eyes is a memory I'll take to my grave.

I told myself such people were entitled to their opinion and they could voice their opinion when election day comes. I tried my best to not let my imagination take flight over what lengths such twisted souls might resort to in order to keep someone like me from exercising my right to seek elected office in the land in which I had become a citizen. Or to serve in office, should I be elected.

But the psychological grenades they tossed my way did take their toll. Letters arrived when my views were aired on TV news footage or in the newspaper following an interview or forum. "Liberal pig!" they would say. The volume of such missives increased after I began attacking my opponent on TV, in the Channel 5 debate and in my ads. It prompted some people to try to jump in between us. It was obvious they didn't appreciate my offensive strategy. And many more people seemed to be buying into his mudslinging — his radio ads claiming I hadn't voted in recent local elections, and the repeated harping on my foreign accent via sound bites.

On the other hand, there would be letters containing $10 checks with a note to the effect: "I saw you on TV and it seems more people like you should be running for office. I don't have much money but whatever I can do to help you I will. Here's my check. Please call me."

Nevertheless, it always gave me a chill to open the correspondence that came to my post office box, instead of my home address. If someone wanted to communicate with me openly, personally, initiate a dialogue, they'd make the small effort to locate my address and write to me at my home. My address and phone number were public information, as part of the campaign disclosure rules. They had been listed in the newspaper. And these letters were invariably warm.

Every day I'd pick up my mail at the post office. The campaign contributions came in self-addressed envelopes my campaign headquarters had mailed out with my logo. But when I'd get envelopes with handwritten addresses, I'd sometimes hesitate. The negative letters were often harsh, though rarely would one get abusive and threatening.

I have long known that people who send hate mail — or make crank phone calls, for that matter — are merely seeking attention. But in the back of my mind I still contemplated what a Women's Campaign Fund consultant from Washington, D.C., had said when she came to Reno to speak with Nevada women candidates.

"I know," she said, "you're missing an incredible opportunity. Because if you would make it known publicly — if you play that right — you could win the election."

This comment had made me feel small, indeed. How could I win an election by victimizing myself like that? I was supposed to cry about being a Latina and that someone was trying to do away with me? Even the thought of making such an attack humiliated me. This was politics? It had nothing to do with the real issues!

I was slowly realizing that I was definitely more naive in this game than I had ever dreamt. The aggressive instinct to win at all costs simply was not in me. What's more, the fear I had for my safety and that of my family was no trivial matter — not material to convert into currency for political gain.

To this day — as I write these words — my son still has nightmares. It is the same bad dream. He still believes someone is going to come through the door of his bedroom. He'll be crying in his sleep. John and I have to stay there with him and repeat that everything is okay and nobody will come to hurt us.

For three months I had refused to let my own apprehensions show. I wanted no one to worry about me. I was far more concerned with ensuring that my son, and my entire family, felt safe.

Meanwhile, I had taken steady precautions. I wouldn't even go out at night alone to get a cup of frozen yogurt. As soon as the sun went down, I was inside or made sure someone was accompanying me, even if I was only driving down to the corner store. I simply avoided taking chances.

It dawned on me one day toward the end of the campaign that this city that has been my safe home for more than 20 years had suddenly become fraught with danger. For somebody like me who has seen so much violence and death, threats like this could not be taken lightly. But on the other side of the tremendous fear, I kept telling myself that this was the land of the free and nobody could or would stop me from running for office.

At night, when I would get into my car after a function and someone would rush after me, my knees would shake violently until I was assured it was some supporter or well-wisher.

One night I sat on Jonathan's bed. It had been the first time in weeks I'd had the time to give him a bath, put him in pajamas, then sit with him to tuck him in.

He asked if I was afraid. I said yes, I was. I was not only afraid someone could hurt me, but I was afraid to become a senator. I didn't know if I could be a good senator.

Jonathan said he had to confess something that was incredibly bad.

He said, "Well, I always, deep in my heart, wish that you'll lose your election. I know this is really bad for you to hear from me, but I wish more than anything in the world that my mommy will lose. And I don't care if kids make fun of me at school, and I don't care if they say you're not good and nobody voted for you. But that's the thing I wish the most. I do not want to live like this anymore."

And that was what was going on in the little world of a six-year-old whose mother was running for office.

Cristina, too, became very protective of me. Sometimes at night, if I hadn't parked my car in the garage and I needed to get some pamphlets or whatever from it, she would walk out with me. She would accompany me to campaign headquarters, anywhere. And she never once went to sleep before I came home.

For John's part, he always has held himself to be a strong person who doesn't ruffle easily and keeps everything in perspective, in balance. As his wife, I sensed he took the initial phone threats as a challenge. He was determined we wouldn't back out.

"The hell with this!" he said. "You're going to file, and we're going to work so hard you're going to win this election." Whoever was trying to stop me they were going to eat their words.

And that set the tone for how we dealt with the hostility, enmity and slimy subterfuge directed towards me over the course of the campaign. Hate letters, threatening phone calls, stolen campaign signs, invective from people whose doorbell I rang — it all ground me down. But I refused to let it crumble me.

The funny thing was, the closer to election day I got, the more resilient I grew. It was like I could endure a little more each day, knowing, "Gosh, we're almost there."

I kept my mind focused on the finish line.

My opponent began his attacks against me on radio and TV as we reached the four-week stretch.

He had aired TV commercials as the anti-crime candidate — walking in his three-piece suit at the simulated scene of a violent crime, ducking gingerly beneath yellow tape (to not muss his hair) then saying, as fake sirens wailed in the background, "This has got to stop." Later, he added a new wrinkle to his anti-crime commercial by subtly casting me as the villain.

But this commercial had backfired to a large extent, serving only to paint him as a racist. In the commercial, he railed against the terrible waste of tax dollars spent incarcerating "illegal aliens." His indirect message was that if voters elected Emma Sepúlveda — "one of them," so to speak — we should expect even more damn Latinos getting arrested and ending up with free room and board, for I would open the borders.

People started calling my home saying how disgusted they were with his commercial. When I finally viewed it myself, I was outraged.

We attacked him, too.

We took issue with his claims that he hadn't raised taxes. We reviewed his voting record. It was a fine commercial. With a guitar playing gently in the background, the camera took a close-up shot of a yellow piggy bank. Then a man's voice said:

"This career politician likes to call himself a fiscal conservative. However, his voting record tells the real truth."

The figure "341" flashed on the screen.

"Three hundred and forty-one times he voted to raise the taxes and fees we pay. That adds up to over 28 tax and fee increases for each of the 12 years the senator has been in office.

"My opponent, fiscally conservative — or the truth?"

Here a hammer smashed the piggy bank to bits. A hand with a Rolex and a diamond ring reached into the mess to pick up a coin.

"My opponent. If he's elected, he'll vote to take your last

dime."

In these final four weeks I met extensively with special-interest groups. I had a long meeting with the Reno deputy police chief. Years before, I had collaborated with two other professors at UNR on a book to teach useful Spanish to police officers and others in the legal profession. I had also been an instructor for Reno police officers and, in order to learn of the police's needs, I had gone on several ride-alongs in patrol cars.

Now I went on ride-alongs again. I needed to know the true crime situation in the city. But it seemed whatever I planned to do in those final few weeks, somehow my opponent found out about it and beat me to the punch. When I climbed into the back of the car for my ride-along, the officer I was to accompany told me my opponent had gone on a similar excursion the day before.

The trip only served to confirm my concerns about the social needs of the community. The areas we patrolled were heavily Latino: Northeast Reno, Neil Road, Robinhood Drive. Driving on Friendship Lane, the ironically named street in Northeast Reno, filled me with a sense of helplessness and sadness. The tension was palpable.

The trip also impressed upon me the dire need for more police officers and more funding for training. Many times the language barrier prevented them from knowing how life-threatening a situation could be. A dispatcher would misinterpret or not understand a phone call, and send officers unknowingly into a danger zone because they didn't speak the language of the neighborhood residents. And there wasn't money to hire more bilingual cops.

And so police would end up watching gunshot victims dying on a sidewalk and witnesses wouldn't even be able to communicate vital information to them. And crime would continue to rise, matters veering out of control. And there was little to nothing a person like myself could do to reach out and help these people.

But I still entertained the notion I could get elected and then make some positive changes.

Meanwhile we were treated to my impeccably clad opponent pontificating on TV in yet another commercial that he was anti-crime, that he supported "one strike and you're out," declaring, "This has got to stop!"

Inevitably, the final week arrived.

A few days before the election, Jonathan told me he was very afraid. He felt something was going to happen to mommy before election day: "Remember mommy what they told us on the phone."

I went to pick him up at school. The radio was on. I wasn't even aware that my opponent's commercials were now airing around the clock. Sometimes the candidate herself is the last to pick up on these things. Jonathan got into the car. Then we heard a man's officious-sounding voice:

"What has Emma Sepúlveda done for this community? Who *is* Emma Sepúlveda?"

My first instinct was to change the dial so Jonathan wouldn't have to hear me ripped apart on the air. But my curiosity got the better of me. I wanted to know what more was being said about me now.

"Emma Sepúlveda . . ." — the roar of a jet engine swelled — "probably has jet lag from flying back and forth to her home in Chile."

The tirade continued. "What has she done for our community?"

Then the voice rattled off my opponent's achievements, from creating the office of consumer advocacy to turning around a bankrupt State Industrial Insurance System, etc.

The knot in my stomach wrenched so tightly I could barely stand it. I knew hundreds of people were listening to this propaganda. And the ad was playing over and over again. He had waited until the final days to broadcast this smear. He was dumping huge sums of money so there would be no way for me to counter the distortions.

How was I to get the truth out? That I had visited Chile once in the past three years. That I was far more committed to my community than my opponent, who hadn't walked the district and who no longer even made his primary residence here in Reno, in his district that elected him.

I left the radio on, as if the ad had been no big deal. I told Jonathan it was a dumb joke, that no one had even heard it. Before we got home, though, a second negative ad came on. This time it was a woman's voice, feigning outrage.

"She didn't vote in the last election," the voice said. "Her name first appears as a registered voter in Washoe County in 1990, and she had to re-register to vote in 1994 in order to run for political office."

In truth, I had registered to vote in the county in 1978, after I became a U.S. citizen, and had voted in 1980 under my first married name. I'd moved to California in 1981, but I re-registered to vote in Washoe County — under my legally regained maiden name — in 1990. I'd voted that year. I missed the 1992 election — not because I had flown off to my "residence" in Chile, but because I was in Chile while I was working for a week as an interpreter/translator for a Stanford University medical doctor working on a case in Latin America. We didn't arrive back in Reno until the day after the election — I heard news of Clinton's victory as we flew over the Andes — so that same year I mailed in a new voter registration card to maintain my registration after missing the election.

To Jonathan's six-year-old mind, his mother was being made fun of on every radio station every five minutes. It was impossible to convince him that these were infrequent ads, airing when few people even had their radios turned on, and few would believe the ridiculous charges, anyway.

This senator was just a real, real bad guy, he said. He was very mad with him. He told me that he wanted to call him and ask him to stop it immediately.

When we got home, Jonathan said he needed to talk to me. His approach is always to call you into his room, sit down and talk to you. He sat down on his bed and started telling me that I should have never, ever gotten involved in running for the senate.

"I wish I had a normal mom," he said. "Not one who is always on billboards and TV. I hate that, Mom. Everybody is going to make fun of me at school because all my friends are listening to the radio now."

He wanted a mom like all his classmates had. Then he started crying. He couldn't take it anymore, he said. He wished the billboards would come down and no one would see me anymore on TV and no one would stop me to talk when we went to the supermarket.

I tried to explain that the race would be over in only a few more days. But that terrified him even more.

In Jonathan's little mind, election day signified The End, when something terrible was going to happen to Mom. He wanted me to drop out of the race that very day, and then things would be okay again. He cried most of that night.

Looking back, the one questionable ad I shouldn't have broadcast was the result of poor advice I'd accepted from a Democratic state senator who told me to take on my opponent over the issue of Honey Lake.

Some wealthy landholders just across the California border, in conjunction with land developers in Nevada, had sought to export water from the small lake into the parched rural valleys north of Reno, with Washoe County picking up the tab. Northern valley residents, fearing a wholesale invasion of their rustic terrain, had opposed the idea as a cheap ploy to justify more subdivisions. Two county commissioners had backed the plan, $13 million was spent to study the idea, but it had ultimately bogged down over the failure to finish an environmental impact study about its effect on the lake and surrounding habitat, and the failure to finalize cost estimates which could have meant an even greater bill to the county.

I had poured over reports and articles about the Honey Lake

water importation project, and had found only one small piece of ammunition to use against my opponent. In 1989, he had supported a bill that would have allowed counties to transfer in water across existing utility lines. But my opponent had voted against the Honey Lake Bill to authorize importing the water when it went before the Legislature in 1993. In truth, I didn't believe it was significant enough to develop into a negative ad. But the Democratic state senator had put a lot of pressure on me to follow through. At a party fund-raiser, he screamed at me in front of everyone, calling me a "chicken" for not taking my opponent to task over Honey Lake.

It ended up that we did make a commercial linking my opponent to Honey Lake. It was poor judgment on my part. It was a weak attack that damaged the credibility of the other attacks I had made.

A reporter did a segment on his morning news show about the lack of truth in campaign ads. He pointed out my opponent's unfounded railings against my voting registration. But he also showed that my opponent really hadn't supported Honey Lake.

In hindsight, I should have hammered unremittingly at the fact that my opponent didn't really live in Reno any more, that he had no business running in the district. After all, not living in the district disqualified a candidate from running. I did not challenge him on this issue and I certainly didn't expose this enough.

That's one way elections are won or lost.

But the main factor — as I found out — was who could make the greatest splash at the very end.

Because the poll only weeks before election day had shown my opponent leading me 34 percent to 30 percent — with 30 percent undecided — his people went crazy in the final few frenzied days before the vote. They sent out no fewer than five mailers to voters in the last week. And not merely to Republicans — but to everybody.

They were slick, oversized mailers. He was spending an incredible sum of money to get re-elected. I received two different mailers in one day: one harping on crime, another appealing to senior citizens.

I had a sinking feeling. I was losing ground fast.

The stakes were raised even higher. His staff must have figured out that I used Plumas Street to drive between my home and campaign headquarters.

On the Sunday before Tuesday's election, Plumas had been blanketed with his signs in people's yards.

What was going on? Had these people suddenly decided at the last minute to commit to my opponent? There, on a corner of Plumas and a side street, a two-sided sign had been placed facing both directions of traffic, outside the business office of an architect I knew very well. He was a Democrat, and had refused to put one of my signs up, saying he didn't believe in political slogans.

I was alarmed. Had even my supporters turned against me? Or had my opponent's staff decided to crank up the heat another notch by planting signs on my driving route without getting permission?

I continued on to my campaign headquarters. I picked up the phone and called my friend. I said, "I know you're a Democrat. And I know I walked by your house and asked if I could put a sign on your property, and you refused. How could you dare do this to me, putting my opponent's sign outside your office when you know I drive past it every day?"

"What?" he said, sounding incredulous.

"You're kidding," he said. "I would never have a sign for anybody outside my business. You know I don't believe in political signs."

"Well," I said. "Do me a favor. Go out and look."

"Hold on," he said. "You don't know what you're talking about."

He put me on hold. He came back on the line, totally out of his mind.

"Who the hell do they think they are?"

When I drove home that afternoon, the sign was gone. So were a fair number outside other Plumas Street businesses and homes.

The eve of the election arrived, charged with anxiety. I felt like I should be doing something, but I didn't know what. A part of me said to relax, leave the vote in the hands of destiny. Another part of me said the time had arrived to do something constructive every single minute, to burn up all my remaining energy so that I could pull off the win.

That's the desperation that takes hold at the very end. Like the marathon runner believing he should push himself to the limit with a flat-out sprint to steal victory.

I couldn't just stay in bed. The phone rang constantly. People who wanted to know more information on where I stood on the issues. People who asked if I had heard the latest election update on the radio. People assailing my opponent for his villainous ads. A constant barrage of calls.

Late that night, my closest staff and friends gathered at our house.

We blew up yellow and blue balloons. It was a rainy night. We went out in the weather and hung balloons on every single one of our signs across the town — hundreds and hundreds.

It was cold, wet and windy. I was tired, hungry and soaked. I'd climb back into the truck to head off for a new destination. And from the radio, that now-familiar man's voice would be saying: "What has Emma Sepúlveda done for this community? Who *is* Emma Sepúlveda?"

It was depressing.

I cried under the rain putting balloons on every one of my signs. I drove through the streets of my district for the last time praying for the misery to end and hoping that those people in so much need would be represented one day by somebody who truly cared about them.

My opponent, it turned out, was the only candidate running for state office who continued to air negative ads on the eve of the election. Everyone else had honored the tradition of switching to a last-minute positive vein, reinforcing that they were the right choices.

Not even Gov. Bob Miller, locked in a bitter campaign against Republican challenger Jim Gibbons, a state assemblyman, had bashed his opponent at the end.

My opponent, it seemed, was determined to leave a bad impression of me in the minds of the voters, instead of a good impression of himself.

This woman is not from here, she keeps jetting back to Chile, she doesn't belong here, and she doesn't vote. He harped on this, over and over.

It was working.

We labored late into the night fastening the balloons. I was exhausted. At the same time, I felt so hyper and sad, I knew I wouldn't be able to sleep.

The knot in my gut had now taken over my whole body.

I spent the night restless, lying in bed, or sitting next to Jonathan's bed, watching his face as he slept. Did he deserve what his mother had put him through for so many months, without even asking him about it?

You're right, Jonathan, I thought. Maybe Mommy's not going to win. And you'll be a happy boy after all.

I turned in at 3 in the morning.

I rose very early and dressed. It was the last campaign suit I would wear.

We woke up Jonathan. He asked me not to take him to school. He wanted to spend the day with me.

I refused. He'd be better off in class with his friends; he'd only be more apprehensive tagging along with me, as I'd be meeting with people, being interviewed by the media, etc.

I told Jonathan he could come and vote with me so he could see it wasn't dangerous, that everybody did it. We drove to the polls at the nearby church. The TV news crews were on hand. John went into an adjacent booth while Jonathan came inside the booth with me.

Jonathan could read by now. We held hands and he read the

names aloud as I punched the holes. He held the silver marker as we pushed the paper circle next to my name. He closed his eyes and told me that he had a wish that he could not tell me. He only repeated, "I wish, I wish. . ." At one point, I punched the hole next to the name of a Republican friend, Brian Sandoval, who was running for the state Assembly.

As we walked out, Jonathan said in a loud voice: "Mom, I cannot believe you voted for a bad guy from the Republican party."

The TV cameras were right on top of us. I prayed they missed Jonathan's quote.

It was hard leaving Jonathan at school. John and I walked him to his class and stayed a few moments, talking to his teachers. He insisted he come home with us. He cried a bit. His teachers told him everything would be okay.

"I promise you, no matter what, I will pick you up at 3," I said.

"Oh, you'll be too busy today," he said.

In truth, I didn't know what to do for the rest of the day. It was one of the most awkward days of my life. My whole destiny was in the hands of people I hardly knew, and who knew so little about me, and half of what they knew were lies.

I went to campaign headquarters. John, David and I went to lunch. They seemed upbeat about our chances of winning. But I think John was starting to entertain serious doubts that we were going to win, although he wouldn't accept them.

Deep down, I was the most pessimistic. Finally, on this day of the election, it hit me: the negative campaign my opponent had generated in the 11th hour had done the trick for him. It had really affected me, and I knew that was a sign that it had far more greatly impacted the thousands of voters who didn't know me.

One of my opponent's commercials had featured a sound bite of my voice, probably taped at the Soroptimist debate, zeroing in on one of the words in English I have difficulty pronouncing — "astonished."

Then the narrator continued, "Who is Emma Sepúlveda?"

The message had surely sunk in: who was this lady who had never done anything for this community, and who kept flying back to her home in her native country, who was a Latina and foreign-born with an accent, running for office here?

If this propaganda was affecting me — making me feel like an outsider, causing me to question whether I had really made a contribution to my community, or to wonder how I would fare with my thick accent were I to serve in the Senate — what effect was it having on the general public?

When we picked Jonathan up later that day from school, the first thing he wanted to know was whether the vote we made for me in the booth would count since he had helped me push the marker.

"Remember, I do not want you to win," he said.

The rest of the afternoon flew by in a blur.

Radio reporters called. The Reno daily newspaper sent a photographer to take several photos of me with my family, on the chance I would emerge the winner.

It was hard to keep a smile on my face. Inside, I felt destroyed.

All that work, all those sleepless nights, all the times I had neglected my profession, my son, my husband — it had been a year out of my life, for nothing.

I went into my bedroom and tried to sleep. It was impossible. The house was filled with people. The telephone kept ringing. Friends. Supporters. My family and friends from Argentina and Chile.

Bouquets of flowers were being delivered from friends both locally and out-of-state, who included notes congratulating me on running a good campaign and assuring me that I was going to win.

I felt foolish for having put myself and those around me through this ordeal. I felt increasingly ashamed. But I had to conceal my feelings, for my house buzzed with excitement.

That evening we went en masse to Taj Mahal, an Indian restaurant on South Virginia Street. I wore a black dress and a bright red jacket and I put on a big golden sun necklace.

I was determined to behave as though I were the winner.

After dinner, we went to the Clarion hotel-casino toward the other end of Virginia Street, where we had booked a suite for our election party. Everybody showed up from the campaign, as well as other campaigns. Elected officials stopped by, too, popping in early to greet me on their rounds. We had two telephone lines into the suite, as well as individual cellular phones and a TV to monitor precinct results.

My opponent took a comfortable lead at the very beginning. He was ahead 56 percent to 43 percent. The margin held steady through the night.

I took it in stride. But John was devastated. Jonathan was having a ball.

"I know you feel bad, Mom," he said. "But you know I am happy."

The three local TV stations sent camera crews and reporters to the suite. I wore my biggest smile. I refused to give any indication that I was defeated. The Channel 8 reporter said, "Are you willing to declare your election loss?"

"No," I said. "We can still have a surprise. I ran a very good campaign and I think the voters realize I'm thinking about the next generation and my opponent is only thinking about his next election."

I wasn't ready to give it up for dead. Too many people had helped on this campaign. Too many happy faces were in the suite. I couldn't let them down.

Little by little, though, what started as a big celebration began to sour. People began to leave the party.

The momentum picked up.

Over and over, sad faces came up to me and said, "You ran a great campaign. You have to do it again."

David, my consultant, said he was totally shocked and surprised. But he conceded that what I had told him the day before was proving true: The anti-immigrant sentiment in America at that moment, and the conservative backlash that was putting Republicans in power at the state and federal level across the nation, had killed any possibility of me winning in 1994.

As soon as the results were shown to be conclusively in my opponent's favor, John couldn't handle it anymore. He left, taking Jonathan home.

Later that night, with most of the precincts reporting, unofficial totals showed that out of 29,000 registered votes in District 4, my opponent tallied a bit more than 8,000 votes, to my approximately 6,000. A few thousand more had chosen "None of the Above" or not voted in the race, and several hundred had opted for other parties.

I acknowledged to those remaining in the suite that I had lost. All that remained was to call my opponent and concede. Several elected officials, including Jan Evans, suggested the moment was ripe for me to pick up the phone and call my opponent and congratulate him.

I lifted the receiver.

In a flash my mind reviewed the past few months. Everything suddenly snapped into perspective — what I had suffered, what my family had suffered, what my friends had suffered, all the brutal attacks my opponent had orchestrated during the last weeks and days of the campaign. How could I be so cynical, so hypocritical, to call this man who I had disliked so strongly for so long, and congratulate him?

I set the receiver back down.

It was 2 o'clock in the morning. The last hangers-on were leaving the party. Some of my friends said they didn't want me to drive home alone. But it was funny. It seemed that all the fear of the past few months was gone. I said I'd be fine.

Actually, I wanted to drive home alone and feel free again.

I was the last one to exit the room. I took the elevator down. I walked alone to my truck.

Strangely, I felt no apprehension that someone was following me, or spying on me, or lying in wait for me. I felt incredibly light.

The tears streamed down my cheeks. And I cried like I have never cried in my life. I cried with deep pain but with a sense of relief and freedom.

I had been a slave in a political fight for people, the majority of whom did not want change. Now I was on my own again, free.

I walked through the cold. The November chill cleansed me.

I walked to my old freedom.

I sat for the longest time in the breakfast nook at home, staring out the window into the inky black.

What did it mean to lose an election when I had seen Mom die excruciatingly from cancer, and Dad disintegrate not long after from the same disease?

When I had seen my own two brothers die under such regrettable circumstances? When I had seen people gunned down by machine guns in the streets of Santiago?

When I had heard the experiences of so many women who had survived unspeakable abuses, struggling year in and year out for any shred of news about their husbands, brothers and sons who were "disappeared" under the dictatorship?

When I had to leave behind forever the land that saw me born?

Losing an election was absolutely nothing compared to any of that.

I considered how privileged I was to be able at least to represent so many people at the polls, to have received 6,000 votes. Votes that meant real trust in building a better society for everyone, including the humblest of the poor. That meant real faith in the future of our democracy, our country, my country. The country to which I have given my new life.

I opened the back door and walked into the back yard. It was deathly silent. The dog was asleep. The chickens were asleep. I could hear only the faint rush of wee-hour traffic on Moana

Lane.

I felt like a prisoner freed from behind bars. Like a political refugee finally making it across the border. I knew now exactly how such souls felt at those life-changing moments.

If I could only scream as loud as I could: "This is over! I am free! Forever freeeee!" But I didn't want to wake John or Jonathan. That would be miserable — for them to come awake suddenly thinking that here at the close of the campaign, something terrible had finally happened to me!

I breathed in the frigid night air as deeply as I could. I filled my lungs. I exhaled and lifted my arms to the mysterious, moonless sky.

The knot in my belly completely dissolved.

I stood looking up at the sky until my uncontrollable tears turned into a peaceful cry of calm resignation. I had my life back in my hands again.

A few days later, John, Jonathan and I went to a basketball game at the University of Nevada, Reno.

Before the tip-off, the announcer declared over the public-address system: "Tonight we have 6,000 people in attendance." And while a beautiful voice sang the National Anthem, I stood up and holding my son very tight to my body, I looked around the arena at the sea of heads. I fought back my tears.

My God. That was a hell of a lot of people.

From Border Crossings to Campaign Trail

AFTERTHOUGHT

Nearly four years have passed since that memorable November 4, 1994. Perhaps ironically, I am certain today that I have accomplished more as a private citizen than I would have accomplished as a single vote in the Nevada Senate.

During these intervening years, I have worked in political campaigns, walked precincts, organized rallies, put up placards and done all in my power to elect to public office people who I believe will work to find real solutions to the problems facing our Latino communities. I have had the opportunity to be Chair of Adelante con Clinton for northern Nevada, and I've founded a non-profit organization devoted to the empowerment of the Latino community through voter registration and voter education: Latinos for Political Education.

The political landscape of Nevada as well as the rest of the country must begin to reflect the diversity of our communities, where citizens of many colors, many voices and many ideologies have a meaningful say in making decisions that directly impact their lives. For this to happen, Latinos must become actively engaged at every level — from schools to churches, from colleges to factories, from private offices to public posts. As we approach the beginning of the new millennium, no one can afford to be apathetic about politics. By not becoming involved, we are in effect allowing the few power brokers to control our communities, our states and, ultimately, our nation.

The problems facing my state today are no different than those I saw when I made the decison to roll up my sleeves and run for public office. Now, however, my approach to solving these problems is very different. I spend most of my 'free' time — time when I am not with my family, working or writing — lecturing and speaking in my community and across the country to civic organizations, groups of concerned citizens, and students from the elementary school level up to the college and university level. My message today places more emphasis on empowering the Latino community through education and participation in the political process by registering to vote, going to the polls every election day and voting.

Losing my run for public office has humbly made me a stronger person, a stronger woman and a stronger Latina. Perhaps most importantly, it has deepened my sense of responsibility and commitment to work to better the lives of Latinos for generations to come.

—Emma Sepúlveda
Reno, Nevada
1998